ALSO BY ESTHER WARNER DENDEL

African Fabric Crafts:
   Sources of African Design and Technique
The Basic Book of Fingerweaving
Needleweaving, Easy as Embroidery
The Crossing Fee: *A Story of Liberia*
Art: An Everyday Experience
The Silk-Cotton Tree (a novel)
Seven Days to Lomaland: *Personal Experience in West Africa*
New Song in a Strange Land:
   Discovering Hinterland Culture in Liberia

Designing from Nature

PHOTOGRAPHS BY JO DENDEL

Designing from Nature

A SOURCE BOOK FOR ARTISTS AND CRAFTSMEN

ESTHER WARNER DENDEL

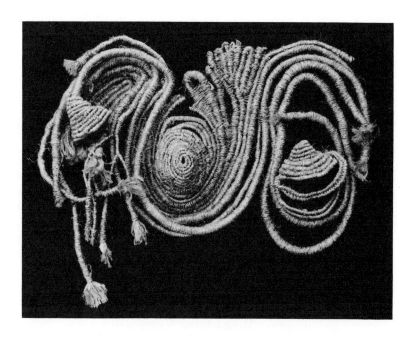

TAPLINGER PUBLISHING COMPANY | NEW YORK

First Edition

Published in the United States by
TAPLINGER PUBLISHING CO., INC., New York

Published simultaneously in Canada by Burns & MacEachern, Limited

Library of Congress Cataloging in Publication Data

Dendel, Esther Warner, 1910–
    Designing from nature.

    1. Design.   2. Nature (Aesthetics).   3. Visual perception.
I. Title.

NK1553.D4   1978   745.4   77–92756

ISBN 0–8008–2173–4 (cloth)   ISBN 0–8008–2174–2 (paper)

Designed by Mollie M. Torras

Contents

Ways of Looking and Feeling

There are many ways of looking at anything. The quality of the light, your mood at the moment, your position in relation to the object—these are just a few of the factors which make for difference. If I look at our rabbit head-on in the flat light of noon, I do not notice his whiskers. If I see him at evening with slanted light behind him, I see a forest of whiskers moving like a wire brush with a nervous tic. The rabbit twitches his whiskers at noon as well as at night. He hasn't changed but the light has, and I have.

Really noticing how the light changes from hour to hour and trying to catch these changes in words makes any day interesting. The interest has to be in me, not in the sky. People say, "That doesn't interest me." They should say, "I have not interested myself in that." As soon as one realizes that interest has to reside inside oneself, not in the thing being observed, the first step has been made toward richer life.

Reading what others have seen and felt and then written about helps me see and feel more acutely. Van Gogh was particularly good at describing sky. When I read in a letter to his brother, Theo, "The sun sheds a radiance of pale sulphur" or "The terrace lit up by a big gas lamp in the blue night . . ." I am able to see sunlight and streetlights with added discernment.

Annie Dillard, who wrote a wonderful little book, *Pilgrim at Tinker Creek,* is an expert at looking and then describing what she has seen. She is speaking of fish in a stream. "Theirs is not the color of the bottom but the color of light itself, the light dissolved like a powder in the water." Or this, "The sky is deep and distant, laced with sycamore limbs like a hatching of crossed swords." One does not need to be a professional writer in order to enjoy searching for words to describe what he has seen. The search concentrates the gaze and heightens the response. I truly believe that there is an intimate connection between the ability to really see and verbalizing the experience.

Poetry is very useful in widening and deepening our response to the world. "Reality involves relationship." Mr. C. Day Lewis has told us that. If we are going to really see, we must see things in relationship. This is poetic vision.

Anything that can alter our habitual responses is helpful. Ralph Waldo Emerson recommended that a man stand in the garden with his head bent over so far that he can see the world upside down between his spread knees. The good of it is that one does not habitually view the world in this posture.

In our culture, the most common way of looking at anything is to see it objectively. This goes back to the ancient Greeks with their great interest in measures and lengths and proportions.

Seeing objectively is only one of several ways of looking. We may take a very subjective approach in which realities are not measured or even measurable, but are intuitively apprehended. We may see with poetic vision, which is to see metaphorically and in relationships that are not immediately obvious. Or we may see abstractly, which offers a special kind of perception.

"Rain Drops," a white and off-white weaving by Doris Fox.

Seeing Abstractly

In case the title of this chapter fills you with apprehension, let me say right off that what I am going to describe is just one more exciting way to view the natural world. It is a special way of looking at things in order to have a direct and immediate perception of them. We separate what we know about the function of, say a leaf, from what strikes us about the leaf when we peer at it intently. For the moment we are

Detail from "Rain Drops."

not seeing it as a little factory releasing oxygen for us to breathe and pulling water from the soil to temper the climate. We have already appreciated all these things about the tree and its leaves. We are looking now for what are called the plastic elements of design which every artist uses whether he is a Sunday dabbler or a great master. (Plastic in this case simply means that which can be formed.) These elements are points, lines, shapes, colors, and texture.

The deeper we get into this the more we realize that a line or shape can "say something" quite independently of what it depicts. The something that it says in its own right, *by its own quality*, is what we are talking about.

Dots "What in the world can a dot *do?*" I hear the question. I am using dots rather than points because a dot is a big point, one big enough to watch. It is also a shape but a special kind of shape. Let's investigate a greasy skillet. The fat has cooled and arranged itself in a pattern of dots floating on water. Physically, these dots aren't going anywhere. The skillet is as stationary as the stove. But as I stare at the dots they seem to be moving. Some are coming toward me, some are going away. Some are moving to the right, others to the left. The dot farthest from me seems to be ascending like a well-filled balloon. It is a tiny little fellow and I feel a great distance from it. The black bottom of the skillet might well be the dark reaches of outer space. Each gob of fat is going wherever it is going visually, not actually. My eyes are supplying the movement. Each dot has a relationship to every other dot and to the edge of the skillet. At the edge next to me a big blob seems to want to slide out of my field of vision. It is swimming out of the picture area which is the skillet.

I notice that I am looking more at the dots near the edge of the skillet than at those in the central area. There seems to be something inside me which I call an instinct for geography. I want to know where things are located in relation to other things and to me. This is an urgent need whether I am looking at a skillet or planning a trip to Afghanistan. The edge of the skillet actually seems to be drawing the nearer blobs toward it. None of the above happens, of course, if you are listening with one ear for the baby to cry or the telephone to ring. It takes utter concentration. If you have never experienced any of these happenings, the first day the dots move for you must be marked in red and shouted from the housetop.

Now with a wooden spoon, I gently urge the blobs near the edge toward the center. At once, I see a configuration my eye can follow. It is like drawing from number to next number in a child's book and ending up with Peter under a flower pot in Mr. McGregor's cabbage patch. Or like tracing out the Big Dipper. There isn't any actual line connecting the stars of a constellation, but the movement of my eyes makes a line *if the points seem close enough to one another to make a path for my vision.*

If I tip the skillet, the dots bump against one another. I don't like the feeling of this; it is agitation and collision. But wait! From the minor tidal wave I created, some dots have slid beneath others. These overlapped shapes create a new shape and suggest depth. I like this happening very much.

While I have been studying my greasy skillet, a couple of hours have sped by, but I don't know this until later. This skillet of mine is a mighty dramatic and dynamic affair.

Instead of grease in a skillet, Beverly Pirtle was the excited observer of mold which formed dots on the surface of a

Stitchery which grew
from a study of
dye pot mold.

pot of vegetable dye. While one is perceiving these dots and feeling the urges to motion which they set up in one's field of vision, one is simply experiencing them. It is after the direct experience that one thinks about them in a conscious way and uses the knowledge which results in the work of art. A stitchery in a hoop was the work which grew out of Beverly's experience of the mold.

Not only mold and grease but anything that floats is worthy of our attention. Oil on water. Bubbles in your bath. Leaves on a pool. Lily pads in a pond. These yield not only dots, but all the other elements of design—lines, shapes, colors, textures.

Lines   When lines meet, they define shapes. If I draw an egg, I bend my line and close it to form an oval. The line is not really part of the egg. It separates the space that stands for an egg from the background space, dividing the "egg" from "not-egg."

In addition to representing objects and acting as a barrier between positive space (the egg) and negative space (the area around the egg), lines have the ability to communicate their own quality. This has nothing to do with what they depict except that a good artist will use a line which underscores the message, if there is one, of his subject matter. If he is drawing fighting cocks, he will use a different line than if he wants to show us swans circling a pool.

What we are after here is a *direct experience* of lines, an experience that pulls at tendons or relaxes one's muscles or tightens the throat or curls one's toes. As with experiencing the dots, this requires complete concentration.

Speed, motion, rest, nervousness, strength, dignity, confusion, serenity—all of these qualities can be communicated by line. Why does a straight vertical line seem dignified, conservative, and stable? Why do we feel pensive under a weeping willow tree? And why is the tree said to be weeping when no moisture falls from it? Why does an elm seem elegant?

When one straight line crosses another at a right angle, the horizontal sometimes seems to be launching an assault against vertical. The place of crossing is a point of attack. Nearly all nonindustrial societies assign magical properties to crossroads. The cross was widely used as a design motif in pre-Christian times. People seemed to feel that the greatest possible tension is created by lines that cross at right angles. The lines seem to crash into one another at the point where they cross. Some ancient designs have diagonals drawn midway between each arm of a cross, and the center seems to pulse like a star. This is the spot. This is the place where vital things happen. This is where the gods are to be invoked. This may just possibly have been how the asterisk had its beginning. To this day the Yorubas of Nigeria call this design a magic square. The arms of the cross point to the cardinal points of the universe and the diagonals to the four corners. You who make this sign are at the center where cosmic forces meet and concentrate.

There is great pleasure in studying drawings by artists who were masters of line. Without the distraction of color, one can respond to the linear quality itself. Some lines run around a figure like a tight wire, quivering with tension. Others bristle with breaks and barbs as though the line had been stabbed on the paper and the rage of its birth lingers on. Some lines flow rhythmically and seem to dance around the shapes they outline. Others are as broken as the speech of a stutterer, but they win us over by their intensity and urgency. When one can look at drawings or at natural objects and experience these qualities, one is truly into the language of line.

Plants "draw" lines by their direction of growth—straight lines, curved lines, bent lines. On the whole nature seems to skimp on straight lines. A spear of grass may thrust skyward, straight as an arrow, but after it has grown a bit taller, gravity curves it back toward its beginning. I know a cypress that makes a dark green mark against the blue sky like an exclamation point turned upside down. Its straightness makes it unique and is the reason I remember it. The straight midrib of a leaf is the only way I can estimate its curvature. Thinking about this gives me a clue to the importance of contrast.

I go to the market, looking for lines. From force of habit I take a grocery cart. Man-made, it is an assembly of metal grids. As I wheel it before me down the aisle, I suddenly see how incongruous it is among the fresh fruits and vegetables.

The curved lines of
milkweed seed floss.

I recall other markets, markets in remote African villages,
markets in Spain and in Yugoslavia, where all the shoppers
carry beautiful, bulging baskets, curved to conform with the
fruits of the earth. They are the color of honey and their
shapes suggest bounty. I wheel the cart back to its nested
fellows.

Bananas are heaped golden crescents, fat little new moons
fallen to earth. I pick up a turnip and stand a long time
admiring the curve of its purple shoulder. A small cabbage
fits in my cupped palms. Spherical melons are stacked like
Civil War cannonballs on a courthouse square. A ruffle of
green lettuce bounds a heap of mushrooms lying like buttons
which have been turned from old ivory. The green husks and
rust silk are peeled back from the tips of the roasting ears.

I think I have found some straight lines. But even here there is randomness. Most of the rows start out to be parallel and straight but fail to keep it up to the tips.

I remember living in lovely round mud huts in the forest villages of West Africa, a memory that stirs to life the sound of rain sleeking down the thatch on conical roofs. As soon as a man becomes westernized, he demonstrates it by building a rectangular house. The builder is advertising that he can think in straight lines. Men from the industrialized nations have taunted the tribal African, saying that he is incapable of using a straight line or the right angle. The ugly new house with its corrugated iron roof is his reply to industrial man.

Straight lines belong to railroad tracks, skyscrapers, superhighways across the prairies, windowpanes, rulers, and a thousand other objects in a technical society. Most hospitals and schools are laid out on a grid. The child is born, goes to school, grows up and works in a factory laid out on a grid. When he finally dies, he is taken over city streets laid out in squares and buried in a cemetery, again laid out on a grid. Man has dominated his world with straight-line efficiencies, including straightened riverbeds. Art provides a way to get off the grid for those who have tired of it. Unless one is designing for machine production, one can indulge what seems a natural preference for the curvilineal. It is difficult to imagine oneself weeping tears shaped like cubes.

Designs made with straight lines, especially when the lines intersect, seem to have been built rather than to have grown. Loom weaving tends to produce lines of threads which cross at right angles whether done in a modern factory or on a simple frame where alternate threads are lowered by strings tied to a button under the big toe of the operator. The "machine," even when it is as simple and primitive as the looms used for the famous Kente cloth of Ghana, presupposes the right angle. Much contemporary tapestry attempts to evade the right angle in outside shape as well as weft direction.

A bent line is one that is curved in part of its length and straight in part. It combines the strength of the one with the rhythm and softness of the other. Too many curves seem sentimental. We have only to look back on the Art Nouveau period at the turn of the century to see this. Can you draw an angular valentine?

Bent lines are a great resource for the contemporary designer. It is a good game to hunt for them among nature's myriad forms.

Sinuous lines of coiling kelp.

The use of bent lines in a design tends to produce shapes which taper from thick to thin. We see this in Jo Willrodt's stitchery, "Mid-Summer." It is built of six layers of fabric, machine-stitched and cut through to expose the various colors.

"Mid-Summer" by Jo Willrodt. (Photo by Margaret Vaile)

On a wall of the old Gobelin workshop in Paris, there is a wonderful vine which I cannot pass without stopping to enjoy. I want to say, "Look, everybody! Don't miss this. Look at the space divisions. *Look at the bent lines.* Look at this vine until you can carry it away in your head."

That is exactly what Bici Linklater has done. In her stitchery on crushed velvet, she has caught the pleasure of sensitive spacing and bent lines and made her own interpretation of growth.

We have a vine on our patio wall which has grown in an equally beautiful way. It is not necessary to go abroad to find one. But there is this about a holiday—one is released from all the rote responses which dull our days and one is more likely to see with fresh vision.

Vine growing on wall of
the Gobelin workshop in Paris.

The vine-inspired stitchery
with raised, padded stems.

When wood weathers in the wind and the sun or is tossed on the tides, the bent lines which are a history of its growth tend to become more apparent.

If a tree is well tended and grows without interference from other trees it will be quite symmetrical (unless that is not its nature as in the case of a twisted juniper). A limb from the liquidamber in our lawn is as round as a tin can and about as uninteresting as far as form is concerned. What we admire in wind-twisted wood is the record of struggle. I would not want to grow old with a face as bland as a baby's.

Weathered wood showing bent and curved lines.

"The gods men worship write their names upon their faces for all to see." Think of that the next time you see a lined old face. As for myself, now that my own face has begun to wrinkle, I note with great satisfaction that it is doing it with bent lines.

Weathered wood which combines curves with bent lines was the source for Rae Kipf's weaving in a hoop. Jute is sturdy enough to hold a sculptural shape and was chosen for this reason.

Working from the same wood, Laura De Lacy made a patio sculpture by coiling sisal. Parts of the sculpture are movable

Weaving based on
weathered wood.

The same piece of wood was
the springboard for this sculpture.

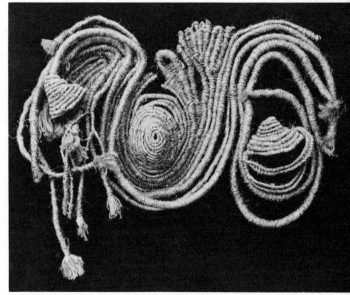

and can be rearranged as one wishes. The sisal was raveled out from leftover scraps of a sisal rug.

Shape   Since grease blobs are one kind of shape, we learned several things about the activity of shapes while we were studying the skillet. We saw that when shapes are close enough together for the eye to move easily from one to the other, they make a path for vision. When they were at this neighborly distance, we may have felt that a sort of hidden tension tied them all together. The tension was in us and we projected it to the dots. We also tried to make a configuration, to group the separate points into a larger pattern. We may have tried to make a closed circuit out of the dot pattern for this is another of the natural acts we do without thinking about it. When the dots overlapped partially, we gained a new shape and a feeling of depth, a new dimension.

One cannot really respond to shapes unless he is able to feel tension, both in a single shape and between groups of shapes. A remarkable book by Sir D'Arcy W. Thompson called *On Growth and Form* goes into the theory that nature's forms result in the balance of the growth forces *within* and the exterior forces *without*. This brings us back to our liquid-amber tree, its symmetry too cheaply achieved for any branch to be interesting as sculptural form.

It helps one to get the feel of tension within and without a form to partially blow up a balloon. The tension within comes from the pressure of air on the membrane of the surface. If you poke it here and there with your fingertips, you change the contour with external pressure.

We have used both *shape* and *form* in our discussion. *The American Heritage Dictionary* gives one word as a synonym

for the other, indicating that they can be used interchange-
ably. However, many artists prefer to use *shape* when speaking of flat pattern and form when referring to the third dimension. I have a print dress patterned with a design of daisies.
The daisy shapes are positive and the area around them negative space. When I wear the dress, it takes the *form* of my
body beneath it.

When I ask my students to tear a simple, beautiful shape
out of newspaper, they invariably ask for guidance or "some
rules about it." I explain about shapes being the result of a
balance between internal and external pressures, and that it
is something one has to feel, not learn rules about. This is the
time to bring out the balloons.

A tray of newly baked sugar cookies lies on the kitchen
counter. They are almost uniformly round except for one.
Little brother has taken a bite out of that one and hastily put
it back. He has made a dented shape. Which cookie does your
eye find the most interesting in shape?

A profusion of mushrooms springs up on our lawn after
a rain. They are very symmetrical when they first appear, but
after a day or two they lose their pristine original shapes.
Holes appear in the tops. Something seems to have nibbled
the rims. They have become *pierced* shapes and *dented* shapes.
Ants have been about their business. Dew has weighted the
top surfaces and the fragile flesh has split. Each mushroom
has acquired a lot of history in the few hours of its existence.
When the growths were new and perfect, I looked at them with
some interest. Now that they have been through happenings
which have altered them, I find the shapes absolutely fasci-
nating. These fellows have earned the beauty I see in their
honestly distressed surfaces. They have lived and they are
still at it.

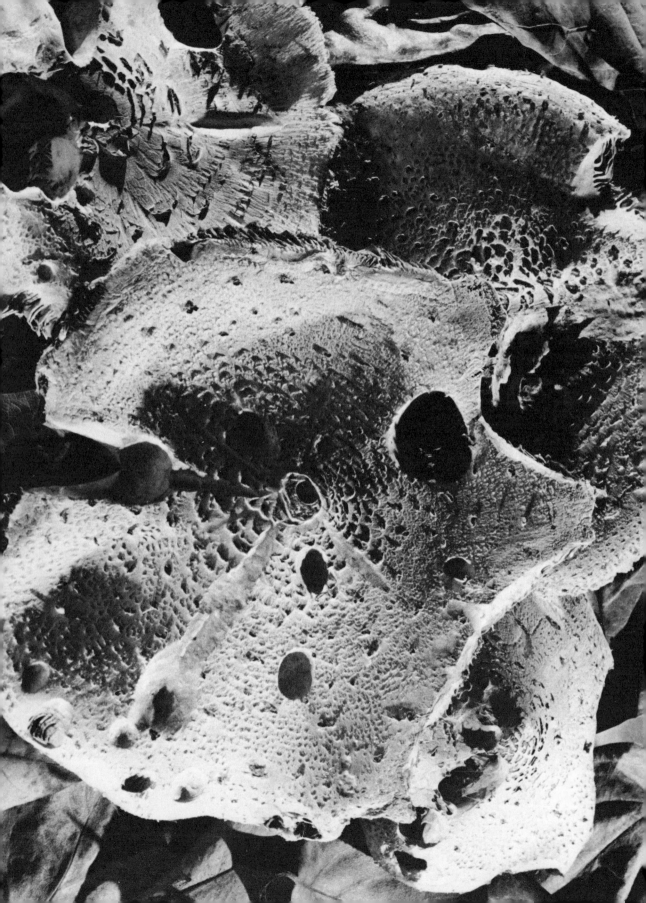

**Mushrooms
with pierced and
dented shapes.**

From studying the mushroom's progress, I learn that I find
pierced shapes and dented shapes and textured surfaces more
to my liking than smooth and symmetrical ones. This is not
a "law"; it is simply the way I feel about what I see. I will
recall this as well as my preference for bent lines when I
begin to design.

Texture   The original meaning of the word texture was "a woven
thing." The skin is aware of the textures that touch it. Even
when we are only looking at a textured surface, we tend to
imagine how it would feel against our skin. We have a strong
feeling for the textures of the things we wear. This strength
of response carries over into the fabric arts and heightens
our response to them.

The textures people enjoy change from age to age. Satin
and pearls and powdered wigs had their own period, a period that seems very remote to us today. We are terribly and
deeply concerned with energy and vitality. Vitality and elegance have always been at war. Our young people feel no
compulsion to make a silk purse out of a sow's ear. They
will wear the sow's ear just as it is, strung with enough beads
to outfit an African shaman. Silk purses, pearls, and sequins
are left for the older generation.

Ours is the denim age. Jeans and T-shirts show up in air-
ports and in good hotels all over the world. Our current need
seems to be to search for what is vital. Hence, bones, feathers, fangs, masks, claws, teeth, skins, fur, and "funky art."
Elegance seems decadent, somehow dishonest. We see this in
the speech patterns of our culture. Our words are earthy,
not elegant.

Moss has been called vegetable fur. When we see it in nature we want to stroke it, to bury our face in it. Sometimes it grows in conjunction with lichens. A patch of brilliant orange lichen against green moss is a dramatic sight. When Bici Linklater thought about how to get this textural appeal into fabric, she decided to use a latchet hook with various handspun yarns and fleece, hooking these into rug canvas. The completed hooking is applied to a pillow.

Yarn and fleece in a pillow cover.

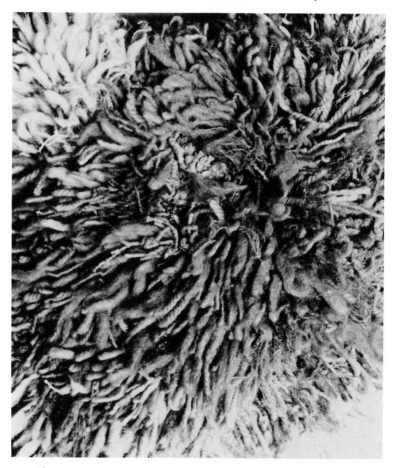

Lichen and moss on a fence post.

A closer view of lichen and moss.

Lichen-inspired hanging by Helen Dickey.

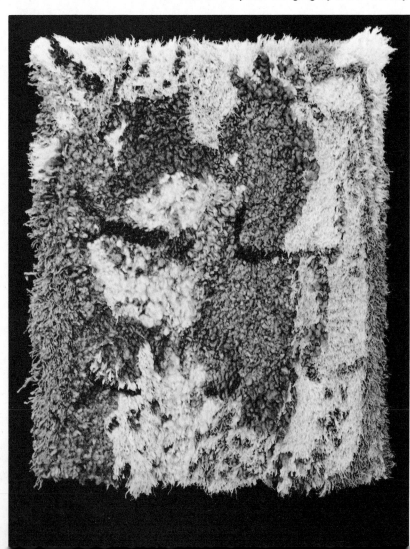

The texture and visual attraction of moss and lichen pro-
voked varied responses from other fabric artists. Helen Dickey
selected fibers of different sizes for a hanging interpreting
a patch of lichen. Her colors are grays and golds with areas
the color of dry straw. She used many threads of natural linen
in her latchet hook as though they were one larger strand of
yarn.

Some other artists responded in weaving and beading. Moss

The relation of
tufts of moss to a
pebbly background
in B. J. Koch's
oval hanging woven
on a hoop.

gave Marian Sanders the idea for a wooden chest which is covered with latchet-hooked canvas in mossy textures. In some areas padded fabric was applied to the canvas and a netting of loose crochet looped over it. Wrapped cords along the edges of the hinges give a feeling of tangled vines.

Moss in fruit growing with lichen formed a beady texture which Pat Wood interpreted in tiny beads for the top of a box.

Much of the charm of old European cities is traceable to the patina which has built up on their buildings over the centuries. We tend to make our modern buildings in materials which do not take on patina, materials like glass and steel. When they get old they are wrecks but not enchanting ruins.

In the wonderful old city of Angers in France is a citadel, parts of which go back to Roman times. Louis I, Duke of An-

Woodsy greens were used in the chest covering
inspired by moss.

jou, moved into the walled castle in 1367 and, to beautify it,
ordered the weaving of the famous and magnificent Tapestries of the Apocalypse. Artists make a pilgrimage from all
over the world to Angers to view the tapestries in the building inside the walls which was built especially for them. The
setting is exactly right. The entrance to the citadel is over a
bridge which could be removed in times of siege. This en-

Archery slit in the citadel of Angers in France. The weathering of centuries has given the walls a patina of great beauty.

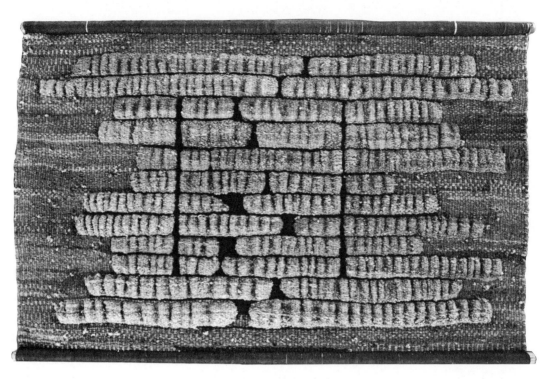

Hanging developed from the citadel of Angers.

trance was guarded by archers stationed in each of the great towers flanking the doorway. Each tower has two vertical slits. The patina on the walls and the weathering around the archery slits were of great fascination to Doris Fox who wove a large tapestry dramatizing the two archery slits and the texture of the wall.

Color   A teacher sets a red apple on her desk and asks her students to draw it. One child picks up a red crayon and draws a recognizable apple shape complete with stem which he then fills in solidly with meticulous little strokes. Another child goes to an easel, dips a big brush in red tempera and rapidly covers an entire sheet of newsprint with dripping red paint.

Color response is intensely subjective. Volumes have been written on color theory, and many elaborate ways of measuring color have been worked out. No matter how much you may learn about color in an intellectual way, your response to it will follow your heart, not your head. It is my own feeling that all the colors in nature are there for us to enjoy. I want to respond to them more than I want to know facts about them. I enjoy knowing facts but I don't get drunk on them. When I look at certain colors, I want to eat them or drink them. I want them inside me; I want to merge with them and be them. "What you see is what you get." Annie Dillard wrote that in *Pilgrim at Tinker Creek*. She tells us that when people who have been blind from birth regain sight through surgery, they tend to see objects as flat patches of color and that all of us saw color this way at birth before we learned about space and form. When she tried to recover this way of seeing, it did not work because she knew the peaches were round; she could not "unpeach the peaches."

It is not only our knowledge of form that keeps us from a pure perception of color. Our second blindness is prejudice. "I love orange but I can't stand blue." Why don't I like blue? A disappointing birthday present I received as a small child was wrapped in blue tissue? Well, something as silly as that. As a result I impoverish myself. I deprived myself of blue in all its possible variety and beauty. All of us need to examine our prejudices seriously.

Ripe olive, salmon pink, mist gray, peacock blue with a touch of black. How does that sound to you? It seemed a revolutionary scheme when Manet painted his "Ballet Espagnol." Even scandalous. I saw those very colors on a blouse the other day. It was being worn by a woman who may never have heard of Manet. No one turned to stare. We are more accepting than we used to be of what were once unusual combinations.

Reading the poets can be a great aid to seeing color more exactly. Marianne Moore will teach you to see frog-gray and duck-egg green. Gerard Manley Hopkins sees a sunset "dappled with damson" and my eyes fill with the image of ripe plums. Snow is not simply something white. It is "wiry and white-fiery and whirlwind swivelled." The milky way is "moth-soft." It is a great game to make up your own unique names for the colors you see.

There are many books on color theory and I have no intention of repeating here what has already been written. I would like to suggest that the best way I know of really to learn about color is to dye fleece, using only the primary colors, red, blue, and yellow, to achieve an endless variety of tones. Keep a record of each combination and a swatch of the result. You will soon find yourself able to distinguish fine gradations of tone in samples which in the beginning seemed identical. The critical eye improves with practice.

Color is seldom seen in isolation. One color can brighten an adjacent color or it can dull it. Relationship again! One could spend his entire life studying the relationship of colors. Nature is the text.

Seeing Objectively

The Sunflower's
Secret
The sunflower's secret is shared by the pineapple, the pine-cone, the chambered nautilus, and many other living things, including man. We call it the sunflower's secret because of the ease with which it can be observed in a sunflower head. If we look carefully at the photograph, we can see that the seeds are set in two kinds of swirls, one curving clockwise and the other counterclockwise. If we held the actual head in our hands and counted the rows, we would see that they are not equal. Most sunflower heads have 34 seeds swirling in one direction and 55 in the other. A giant one grown in the Soviet Union is reported to have spirals containing 89 and 144 seeds.

Now these numbers are not accidental. They represent a ratio which has been called magic, even divine. Their story goes back to the thirteenth century and a man whose name was Fibonacci, although his neighbors called him Leonardo the Blockhead. Fibonacci's first great achievement was to introduce Arabic numbers into Europe with a publication called *The Book of the Abacus*. A small section of the book dealt with the appalling fertility of rabbits. He calculated how many rabbits would be born in a year if a pair were placed in a cage and if, after two months of age, every pair of rabbits reproduced another pair. He listed the number of

38

Detail of a
stuffed and stitched
pillow cover
by Bici Linklater
evolved from a study
of sunflower seeds.

pairs which could be expected at the end of a year and came up with the Fibonacci series which bears his name to-day: 1, 2, 3, 5, 8, 13, 21, 34, 55, 89, 144, 233, etc. Each number is the sum of the two before it. If you will look above at the count of seeds in the sunflower heads, you will see that 34 and 55, and even the Russian giant head with 89 and 144, are right out of the series.

If you wiggle your finger joints to see where they actually bend, you will see that the third or long joint next to the hand is equal in length to the sum of the other two. We carry the Fibonacci series in the measurements found all through our bodies. When this was first noticed, the proportion did indeed seem divine.

Another curious thing about the numbers in the series is

that if you divide any one of them by the next highest number, the answer will be 0.618 or very close to it. It comes out precisely that after the fourteenth in the series. This ratio of 0.618 to unity or one is used by book designers, architects, artists, craftsmen—anyone concerned with making a rectangle of pleasing proportions. It is easy to construct.

The drawings show how to draw the golden rectangle. The right-hand edge of the beginning square is often referred to as the golden slice.

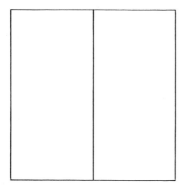

Draw a square and divide the square in half with a vertical line.

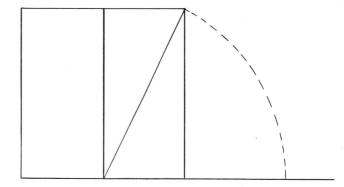

Draw a diagonal through the right half of the square. Take the length of the diagonal in a compass and swing it down to the baseline.

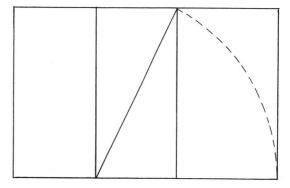

When the length is established, complete the rectangle.

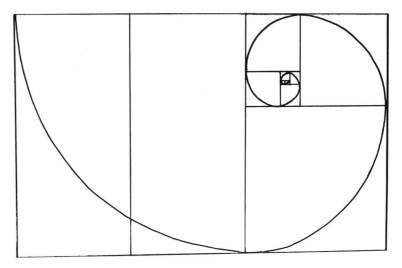

Logarithmic curve.

A unique characteristic of the golden rectangle is that we can take a square out of the minor section and have within this smaller rectangle the same ratio we started with. We can continue this as long as any space remains, without changing the relationship of major to minor portion. This is not true of any other rectangle. For this reason, the shape is sometimes called the rectangle of the whirling squares.

If we draw a curve touching the corners of these successively smaller squares, we have a logarithmic curve. The sliced shell of a chambered nautilus shows how the "stately mansions" of this sea creature are built to logarithmic specifications.

If the only use we wish to make of the golden proportion is to decide on a pleasant length for a certain width, we can do this by arithmetic. Simply decide on a width and multiply that number by 1.619. Thus if we wish to have a weaving 18 inches wide, the length will be 18 × 1.618 or 29.1 inches for a golden rectangle.

Chambered nautilus showing the logarithmic curve
in the growth pattern.

A batik by Peggy Kauffman using the logarithmic spiral.

The tight coil
of a new fern frond
is one of nature's most
beautiful spirals.
Its tension suggests
the boundless energy
of growth.

Plants other than sunflowers spiral in numbers of the series. Study a pinecone to see whether its ratio is 5:8. Check a pineapple for an 8:13 ratio. Look at the center of a daisy for a 21:34 count. Consider that the ideal human figure is eight heads high with the navel dividing the body into a 3:5 ratio. I am using the word "ratio" here instead of "proportion" because a ratio is the relationship between two measures, while proportion implies at least three.

The sunflower's secret is one of hidden geometry, although now that we know it, we may wonder why we needed to be told, why we did not discover it for ourselves. There is a real thrill in recognition when a veiled form suddenly becomes clear. My instinctive response to the Parthenon was greatly heightened by my knowledge that hidden in the facade, which is itself a golden rectangle, there are smaller golden rectangles and that my eye was able to find them. The major and minor parts of a parent golden rectangle are generative, indeed, as their offspring whirl around them.

It has been charged that Americans do not know how to look at great architecture, that a trip through Europe becomes for many of them "just one old church after another." If this is true, perhaps it is because our vast prairies and the long vistas of the West with overarching sky do not provide ratios of width to length to height and that we really are not given, as a people, to the contemplation of proportion. We need boundaries and limits before we can feel relationships of space. We can recover this sense which was so vital to ancient Greece by studying the plants in our own garden. It is tremendously important to me to know the manner in which plants grow.

The stalk of almost any growing plant will furnish evidence of the Fibonacci series. Start at the bottom of the stalk with the first leaf but do not count that one. Move up the stalk until you come to a leaf directly above the first one. If the plant has grown in a healthy way without interference, you will have a number out of the series. The number of times you circle the stalk, regardless of the direction, will be another number out of the series.

We could continue for a long time listing our own discoveries of the series in nature, but it will be more exciting for you to do your own counting and observing. We should mention that nonliving matter seems to form in different systems. Snowflakes have six parts rather than fitting into the series. The relationships in living matter have been called dynamic symmetry, while those in snowflakes and crystals are referred to as static symmetry. These have great beauty, too, but of a different order.

USING THE GOLDEN RECTANGLE IN DESIGN

The first and most obvious use is to obtain a rectangle whose ratio of width to length is satisfying and pleasant. We can also use our rectangle to decide on a pleasing place for our center of interest. If we draw a diagonal of the entire golden rectangle, the place where this diagonal crosses the

Center of interest placement.

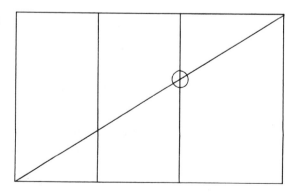

Dyed and bleached fabric
with stitching based on the golden slice.

original square with which we started, the line called the golden slice, will be found a satisfying position for the most important part of our design. The rectangle may be turned to be a vertical rather than a horizontal if desired.

In a stitchery which I did recently, I dyed a piece of pale blue Indian head with potassium permanganate. With a cotton swab dipped in lemon juice, I bleached out lines, drawing, without actually measuring out the space, a golden slice and lines turning about the spot where the diagonal crossed the slice. These lines were then enhanced with stitchery.

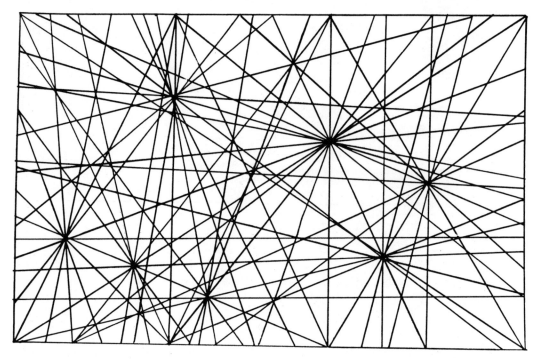

Drawing a golden rectangle grid.

DRAWING A GRID WITHIN A GOLDEN RECTANGLE

Drawing a grid within a golden rectangle is a great game. To begin, draw diagonals of the entire rectangle from corner to corner, in both directions. Then draw diagonals in both directions in each half of the original square and in the added minor rectangle. Each place where two lines cross is called an "eye." From here on, draw through any two "eyes," carrying the lines entirely across the area. Continue until a considerable network has been established. You will notice that some "eyes" become quite prominent and that these prominent ones set themselves up in curves.

The grid design was used by Judy Amsel to superimpose a study of a green pepper. She drew the contours of the bottom

shape of the pepper, repeating and varying these. In order
to make an easy path for the eye to follow, certain areas were
inked in solidly.

If the "eyes" are used for placement of the design motifs,
the actual grid lines may not show in the finished work. In
many of the designs scattered through this book, a grid was
used for placement and then discarded after it had fulfilled
its function.

Contours of the inside of a green pepper
arranged over a golden rectangle grid.

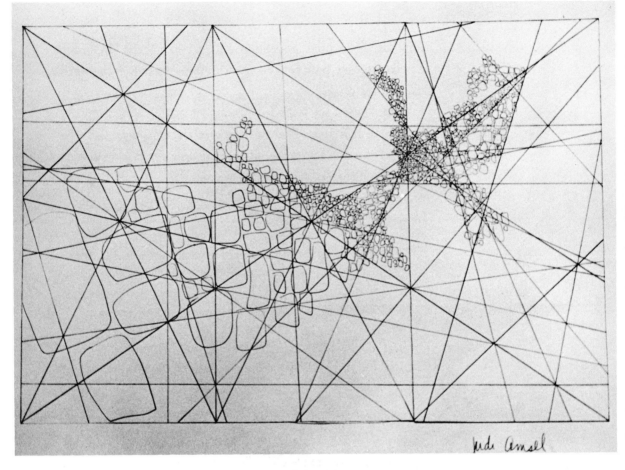

A progression of sizes.

In one of Judy's designs, she started with the idea of making a design based on the seeds of the green pepper. These start very small where the diagonal crosses the golden slice, and gradually become larger as the distance from this point increases. When we work with a progression of sizes, a rhythm is set up.

In doing a cartoon for a weaving based on the tensions in the plaster of a Masai house, I first drew the grid within a golden rectangle. I tore pieces of newspaper to arrive at the shapes I wanted to use. These were then superimposed on the grid with the large flower form placed where the diagonal crosses the golden slice. Other shapes were placed over "eyes" which developed in the grid. When I was satisfied with the arrangement, I stuck the torn shapes down on the grid. The grid lines used in that way give me a sense of security as I design.

Before we leave the Fibonacci series, you must wonder how many pairs of theoretical rabbits there were at the end of one year. Fibonacci calculated that there would be 233 pairs.

Developing the design for
a weaving based on a Masai house wall.

Rabbits can not go on forever, but numbers can. The one hundredth number in the series is 354,224,848,179,261,915,075.

DRAWING A ROOT FIVE RECTANGLE

A rectangle closely associated with the golden rectangle is the root five rectangle. To draw it, construct a square as we did to draw the golden rectangle. Draw a diagonal of *both* halves of the original square as shown on the drawing. Swing both of these diagonals down to the baseline to arrive at the length of the rectangle. It is obvious that this is a golden rectangle with an extra minor section.

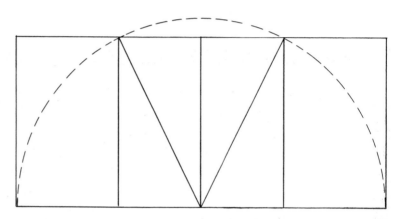

The root five rectangle.

In order to arrive at this length by arithmetic, a width is decided upon and this measurement is multiplied by 2.236 (the square root of five).

A grid may be drawn in this rectangle just as it was in the golden rectangle.

• • •

Some artists feel that the use of dynamic symmetry is too mechanical and mathematical. It is true that it can be used in a lifeless way. On the other hand, what is present in the depths of one's own being and in the world all about is certainly worthy of our attention. If we are unable to feel nature's proportions the fault does not lie in nature. The lengths of the strings of a musical instrument are a matter of mathematics. Knowing this does not detract from my pleasure in a symphony.

Seeing with a Camera A single-lens reflex camera can help one see the world in a new way. Going about with a camera should be a deliberate questing. A marathon of random pointing and clicking seldom yields any new experience, much less a decent photograph.

Looking through a lens isolates a part of what the roving eye naturally sees and concentrates attention on a small area. Moving closer to the object under scrutiny reduces the area being studied. For the moment we lose the rest of the environment and are able to focus all of our attention on a single bit of matter. It is like placing blinders on a horse so he will be able to see only the track in front of him. We all need that kind of aid sometimes.

People without cameras can do something of the same sort by cutting a cardboard frame. Looking through the hole, one finds one's picture. The hole is a window for viewing the world. This kind of looking is a deliberate pleasure, not to be done in a hurry.

For many years after the invention of the camera, photography was thought of as a purely mechanical process. In

1896, there was talk among the members of the New York Society of Amateur Photographers of transforming their organization into a bicycle club. They had "done" photography. A man in his early thirties, Alfred Stieglitz, who had been devoting all of his time and energies to photography, offered to help revive the organization and to publish *Camera Notes*, a photographic magazine. As a result, exhibitions were held all over the world. Stieglitz was determined that photography be recognized as art as great as any of the accepted art forms. For Stieglitz, photography became "an act of vision, of life itself."

In the thirties when I was a graduate student in art, it was the students' great privilege to haunt Stieglitz's gallery where one might see not only the paintings of his wife, Georgia O'Keeffe, but also catch intimate glimpses of the famous couple. It was Stieglitz's habit to charge up to someone looking at an O'Keeffe painting and demand to know, "What does that painting make you feel?" There was great emphasis on the word *feel*, and it was important to make an honest answer. I watched him show people out the door who had tried to equivocate. He was a short man but so intensely vibrating with energy and vitality that he seemed to fill any space he was in. I remember little tufts of white hair sticking out of his ears like the ends of round paintbrushes. Gertrude Stein caught him in words when she wrote, "I felt him having white hair."

This man was important to art students not only because of his camera work, but also because he was the first to bring contemporary painting to the American public's attention. That was the famous Armory Show of 1913. But most of all, he was important to us because he would talk to us, mere students. He wanted us to feel the leafiness of a leaf, the metallic hardness of an automobile hubcap, the beauty of a human hand in all the ways it can bend and clutch and curl, and reach. His life and his conversation revolved around feeling. There was nothing sentimental about him. Everything was real and deep or not at all.

With his camera Stieglitz taught us to look at everyday things, clouds, reflections, sheep, horses, old barns, and trains, in new ways, in feeling ways. All of us are in his debt. Perhaps none of us will ever take a really great picture, but every one of us can find something toward which to offer a deep and honest response, and the camera may well be what helps us find that object. I remember especially a photo of his which showed only part of the flank and the harness of a workhorse. He called it "Spiritual America." Neither harness nor a horse has looked the same to me after seeing that picture.

Whether one is taking a photograph or enjoying one which someone else has taken, the response to the subject should be entirely personal. No one has the right to tell anyone else what to look for or what to see. After several persons have looked and established their own relationship, there is no harm in sharing responses. Sharing is quite different from "being told what." I deeply resent so-called "art appreciation" books which tell me what I am supposed to see and feel when I look at certain paintings. I cannot possibly see through another's lens and I don't want to. The way that I see is slanted by the sum of everything that has ever happened to me. Other and different things have happened to you. For this reason we are presenting without comment two of my husband's photographs which may or may not evoke a response or say something special to you. They were taken in the feeling way which Stieglitz has bequeathed to new generations of artists who believe that photography is an art in its own right. Good photographs do not always come from exotic places. The wilted cabbage leaf came out of the trash can.

Wilted cabbage leaf.

Kelp.

SLIDE VIEWING

Slides are projected in a darkened room so there is really nothing to look at except the image on the screen. This in itself induces concentration on the picture and eliminates distractions. It always surprises me that we see things in the slides which we did not see when the picture was being taken. A good picture, among other things, is a source of information.

Turning color slides gradually out of focus is a great aid to designers who tend to get "locked into" an image and who reproduce it too literally. A very ordinary subject as it begins to blur slightly may take on some of the poetry of an Impressionist painting. Solid forms seem to dissolve and become evanescent patches of color. We begin to see the lyric rather than the banal aspects of the subject. After studying the out-of-focus image, it is good to bring it very slowly back into focus and study the changes in reverse order.

Seeing Subjectively

A remarkable philosopher, Martin Buber, has placed all possible relationships in two categories, I-Thou and I-It. He speaks of a tree. He can see it in any of many ways—as a picture, as a shape, as a structure, a movement of growth processes, as a manufacturer of oxygen, as a species one may classify, as a material one may measure. While one is doing any or all of these things, the tree remains an object and one is looking at it objectively. This way of looking is scientific. It is emphasized in our schools and is commonly considered the correct, indeed the only valid way, to look at the world.

I am not going to say that looking at the world objectively is wrong. I thoroughly enjoy knowing how many gallons of water a large tree pulls up out of the soil in a day. I know of no drawings which seem more beautiful to me than those found in morphology texts. These delineate the form and structure of living things. I like to know the genus and species of the plants I see. It is only when objectivity excludes all other ways of seeing that I object. Emerson has told us that it is a dull observer whose experience has not taught him the reality and force of magic as well as of chemistry. It was a man of science, Sigmund Freud, who called the attention of the world to the fact that there are ways of knowing which are poetic rather than rational in spirit.

We hear a great deal these days about existentialism. There are several varieties of this philosophy. My favorite writer on the subject is Nikolai Berdyaev who perhaps leans a little too far toward subjectivity. Here he defines existentialism: ". . . it is a philosophy which does not accept objectivizing knowledge." He goes on to say that objectivization means alienation, depersonalization, and loss of freedom. Through subjectivity, the I acquires a feeling of kinship and nearness to all living things.

The I who sees the tree in the various objective ways described above may enter into a different, a subjective relationship with it. Relationship takes two. If I have what Buber calls the "grace" to know the feel as well as the look of this tree, I have responded to it in an I-Thou manner. But what of the tree? Buber suggests that in the dim world beneath speech, growing plants as well as animals may have their own responses to an honestly offered Thou.

There is a very important difference between an It and a Thou. All Its are to be used. Thous are to me *met*. Buber calls this possibility for Thou-ness, "the hallowing of the everyday." One need not belong to a certain religion, or indeed to any religion at all, to feel in the depths of his being that eating, touching, talking, dancing, making, mating, are holy acts, each one a sacrament.

To do everything one does with feeling takes time. If an act can be accomplished by habit without thought or feeling, one may become very efficient. And very dead. We perform too many lifeless acts shaped by repetition into habit. Our rhythms have been too feverish.

Meaningless moments and emptiness are the curse of our

age. We are numb, without feeling, when we could be, as Emerson put it, "glad to the brink of fear." Meaning flows back into life with every Thou-ness one can achieve.

Thou-ness does not lend itself to measurement, and we tend to be skeptical about anything we cannot measure. We don't quite believe in a reality we cannot weigh and measure. When Elizabeth Barrett Browning wrote "How Do I Love Thee?" she came smack up against this problem. She starts out mentioning depth and breadth and height in the second line, and the poem is the more powerful for it as she moves on to symbolic dimensions. She loves *to the level of everyday's most quiet need*. Through her poetic skill we are convinced of the magnitude of her love. Love doesn't dole itself out by the pound or the kilo, but it's a reality all the same.

We handle things differently as their Thou-ness comes alive to us. The touching fingers linger, giving time for feeling to flow. The rhythm of life changes as we learn to take time.

I pick up a small, brown, water-washed pebble, not because I want to use it for anything but because I want to experience it. The pebble is as cool as a dog's nose. If I were too warm, I would rub my forehead with this smooth, cool surface. I warm it by cuddling it in my palm. I close my eyes and memorize its form with my fingers. I caress it with my tongue the way animals lap the earth at a salt lick. I imagine that my body is a huge microphone, very sensitive, which can pick up and magnify the sounds of molecules in motion within the stone. We want and need to be in touch with the life-forces of the universe, even those within a stone. The stone is throbbing to the slow rhythms of geologic time, a vibration I can only imagine because it is below the threshold of human perception. I keep and cherish my drab brown pebble.

It is possible to eat food without any sensuous, much less

spiritual experience. We can gobble it down so fast we do not even taste it. If we really want to experience an apple, we must take time to enjoy its color and form before our teeth break the skin. We must turn it in our hands and we must smell it. Ah, the delicious odor of sun-ripened fruit! As we pierce the taut skin, little beads of fragrant juice pop out into the air, scenting the room.

When I was a child, our family saved their money to buy one great luxury each fall—a barrel of apples which was stored in the cellar. Each red, red fruit was wrapped in a square of purple tissue. Every winter night after we had banked the fire in the kitchen stove, we brought a plate of them up out of the chilly cellar. There was no light in the cellar, so feeling for the round, cool spheres was our first experience of them. We sat around toasting our feet on the open oven door while our mother polished each plump red globe with a clean white towel. She would hold each one up to catch the light of the kerosene lamp to see whether its skin glowed wtih proper luster. Before she had finished with this, the cold would be creeping in under the outside doors and finding our shoulder blades through the rungs of the kitchen chairs. A north wind usually pried at a loose board at the corner of the house, a sound we scarcely noticed until the room began to chill. We heard it then and also the loud hum of the tightening telephone wires which connected us to our nearest neighbors. As the stove cooled, we pulled our chairs closer to the oven until chair touched chair.

"The way to make an apple last a long time," my mother said, "is to scrape it with a spoon." And we did. It was a game to see who could make his last the longest. This was partly because neither my brother nor I wanted to go to bed. But it was tolerated because my mother knew we were doing something even more special than eating apples. We were *experiencing* apples. What the fruit gave us in that encounter was a clue to finding the Thou-ness inherent in the fruits of the earth.

Poetic Vision

We asked our African daughter how she would describe snow and ice to her people in tropical Liberia. There is no word in the Mano language to convey the brutal force of the Midwestern winter she had just experienced.

"I will tell them about a terrible *bone of water*," she said. "They have known only water that is soft and wet and flows. I will tell them of water that is hard and sharp and cold. It stings and hurts and there is heat in the hurt. Our old people make needles out of slivers of bone. I will ask them to think of an army of bone needles flying at their faces, points first. This war on the face is called sleet and the needles are the bone of water."

Finding a relationship between *water* and *bone* and *cold* takes a certain slant of thought which comes naturally to African people. We of the Western world have almost lost the ability and we are poorer for it. Long ago when plants and flowers were being named, our ancestors were able to think poetically. A daisy in Chaucer's *Legend of Good Women* was *dayeseye*, or "eye of day." In our time we have trouble naming a cat.

Robert Frost thought that we must get poetry into our high

schools. Young people *do* respond to poetry. Often it is their elders who worry about whether it is "practical." The low esteem in which most of our countrymen hold poetry is part of the very real cultural shock I feel when I come back home after being in Africa.

A poet does not invent relationships; he discovers them. He goes through life searching for connections. We all do. But poets have a tool to use in their quest. That tool is the metaphor. If the poet finds a metaphor that is fresh and unexpected, we respond with pleasure and excitement. A metaphor finds relationships where the casual eye sees none.

We are limited in our search for connection, limited by our knowledge as well as our ignorance, limited by prejudice. But limitations can be useful. The limitations of a tribal language enabled our African girl to build a striking new image. The Japanese have a form of poetry called haiku in which limitations are self-imposed. They limit their haiku to three lines and a total of seventeen syllables, five in the first line, seven in the second, and five in the third. This limitation compresses meaning in a small unit that seems to explode with power when a receptive ear is present. The listener completes and enlarges the haiku by his own associations and memories which attach to the haiku like ripples spreading in a pond, the haiku being the thrown pebble that starts the movement. Usually a haiku makes a reference to a season, the weather, or some other observation from nature. A key word cues the reader into the setting. In a great haiku, the third line suggests the new and often mystical relationship which has been discovered.

The Japanese master Basho, who lived between 1644 and 1694, is considered the best-loved and greatest master of the form. He wrote:

Dry cheerful cricket
Chirping, keeps the autumn gay . . .
Contemptuous of frost

We know that he is talking about something besides the first frost of autumn. He is talking about the autumn of his own life and how to meet death with courage.

Our attempts at haiku may be no match for those of Basho and the other Japanese masters, but that is not important. What does matter is that through practicing the limitations imposed upon us by the haiku form, we may enlarge our relationship with the universe. Very often when one is writing haiku, the significant third line is not immediately discovered. One morning when I looked out of the window I was struck by the brilliance of each rain-washed leaf. Immediately I had the first two lines of a haiku:

Wet leaves mirror sun
What has happened to the dust?

It was several days later that I knew what had happened to the dust and I wrote the finish line:

Layers deep are cleansed

I do not need to say that layers of dust are like accumulated guilts or that my tears are like the rain. Like many things in poetry, these are implied and do not need to be boldly stated.

If you have not tried to write poetry since you were very young, you may be appalled at the thought, defeated before you start. Most of our workshop group were. Those who had the courage to try did better than they expected. Here is a poem by Laura De Lacy which grew out of that challenge.

I am
Just being here.

Just being here,
I am.

I am
More than I am
Just being here.

I like this little poem very much. It shows us the heightened sensibility of an aware person who is deeply in love with the world. The implication is that by being here with a group of beloved friends who meet every week to grow creatively, she is increased in their presence.

One of our group, Joan Coverdale, is an expert photographer as well as a poet. One medium of expression seems to intensify and heighten the other. Enjoy her photograph of kelp, then read her poem.

KELP

Amber fibers
Born of the sea.
Sinuous golden forest,
Stretch for the sun.

Follow the flow,
Form and reform,
Protective pliant barrier,
Calm the sea surge.

Give dimension to depth,
Strength to growth,
Yield,
To the storm.

Kelp. (Photo by Joan Coverdale)

"Bloody Thunder,"
a stitchery.

My friend, Judith Ann Green, the poet, is also a stitcher. "Bloody Thunder" is a little wall stitchery, only $3\frac{1}{4}$ inches by 5 inches. It is meticulously worked in cotton floss on bleach-dyed satin acetate. Here is her poem:

BLOODY THUNDER

The sun went down
    in bloody thunder
Tearing the trees
    from the blue silk
    and dipping them
In orange shrieks and moans
While the pizzicato rain
      punctuated my eyelids
And stitched the night
    to the horizon.

Poets often assign color to sounds. If a shriek is orange as Judith Ann has it, what is the color of a sigh? Or a yawn?

The back of a Levi's jacket is the setting for Judith's "Eclipse." Satin acetate was bleach-dyed so the color runs from a sunset red to gold. Cotton floss, rattail couching, and

"Eclipse," an appliqué on back of a Levi's jacket by Judith Ann Green.

tarred seined twine were used to enhance and pattern the surface. Here is the poem which provided the imagery:

ECLIPSE

> Hand-holding dancing,
> feathered sky father
>   circled
> by night's fat sister
>   laughs aloud
>   from behind.

If writing a poem seems quite beyond you, you may like

to try to interpret the poetry of another in a weaving or a stitchery or a basket.

"Autumn Woods" is an unusual basket by Sarah Pilkington. The sides are a double layer. One looks through trunklike patterns of dark color to brilliant autumn colors on the inside layer. The ends of the jute warp branch out at the top like twigs. Her friend, Mary Hurley, wrote the haiku that goes with the basket:

> Forest foliage flames
> Beyond twisted charcoal trunks
> Autumn alchemy.

"Autumn Woods,"
a basket with double sides.

Ways to Develop a Design

Finding our sources in nature brings unity and wholeness into life for the reason that we are, ourselves, part of nature. We have tried to look at natural objects until our spirit is living within them and we are participating in their life which is as real as our own. We have looked not only at outward shape and color, but the inner structure and concealed volumes. We have not set out to copy natural forms, but to arrive at a oneness with them. We have tried to look at them in every possible way—subjectively, poetically, abstractly, and objectively.

To copy a natural form is nothing more than to make a model of it. The model has the same relationship to the natural form as a store-window dummy has to a living person. Our forming process must be like breathing, a taking in and a giving out. We take in every possible aspect of the natural form and give out something different which has been transformed within us. "The perceptive eye, then the interpreting imagination." This is how C. Day Lewis explains it.

"Why not just enjoy nature and forget about making anything?" I hear that question rather often. There is a feeling that breathing in is just great but that giving out is a bother.

Walt Whitman must have heard that argument and been troubled by it when he wrote:

> Dazzling and tremendous, how quick
> the sunrise would kill me,
> If I could not now and always
> Send sunrise out of me.

A pond which is fed by a crystal-clear spring becomes stagnant very quickly if it has no outlet. Outlets are as important as inlets. They keep the flow flowing.

Our thoughts and dreams become vague and thin out when they are not attached to matter. This pen, this paper, this needle, this shuttle, I *need* them. Not just to keep busy or to fill time. I need them because they are the tools for the outward act of making; they give me outlets for the inlets. Without them I would stagnate. The flow would be blocked.

Now to be practical about it, what *are* the ways we can design using nature as our source? We can explore only a few of them within the limitation of one book. We may repeat a form with variations. We may use only one small part of a form and build on it. We may use all of a form and enlarge it. We may abstract a form until only its more salient features remain. We may enrich a form with line or texture or color until it is quite different from the object which set the project in motion. These are a few of many possible solutions. Let us see how they work.

Repetition with
Variation

I have spent the morning studying a handful of sunflower seeds. They are all the same general shape but every single one is patterned differently. Another thrilling morning I spent on the Serengeti Plain watching a herd of zebra. Each

Sunflower seeds.

one was differently striped. Sometimes I watch a crowd of people picking up their baggage at the airport. Each head is the same general shape but no two sets of features are alike. I place my thumbprint on the application for a driver's license knowing full well that, of all the thousands of thumbs there are in the world, not one matches mine. The variety in nature's repeats is endless. I am back with the sunflower seeds. Which is the most beautifully designed? I cannot decide. Each one is a masterpiece.

Variety in unity. This is our goal in designing. How much variety can there be before the composition visually falls apart? Too much repetition without enough variation is boring. This, I think is the more likely pitfall. If someone sings the same note over and over, it is worse than boring. It is torture. The regular drip of a leaky faucet is an apt example.

Variation can be in size, in color, in texture, in shape, in proportion. In the sunflower seeds, the marvelous variety comes through varying the width and spacing of the dark stripes.

A small rock from the Himalayas was brought home by Maggie Thompson as a memento of a happy trip. The rock is shaped somewhat like an apple turnover and seems to have been molded by giant fingers playing with the rounded edge as one would play with a pie crust. The thinner edge bears the print of fossil sea life. What to do with one single shape to make a composition out of it?

A rock from
the Himalayas.

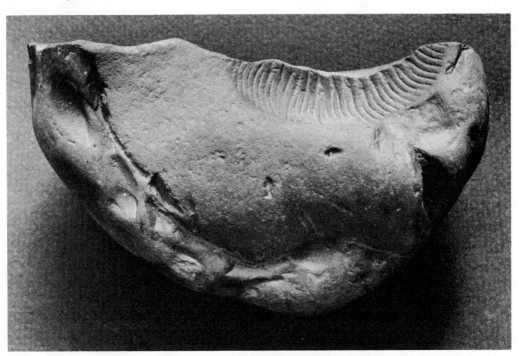

Repetition was the answer. In three repeats, the size is varied for added interest. The fossil pattern is simplified into bars of varying widths. This bar motif is repeated in a subtle way in the background. The dark tone of the background makes a path for the eye around the pleasing rock shapes.

Repetition of shapes is a way to set up rhythm because rhythm presupposes repetition. It can't exist unless something is repeated. Variety makes the melody.

Sections of leaves from the same plant turn and curl and twist to provide interesting variations in their repetition. The

Stitching developed from the Himalayan rock, by Maggie Thompson.

Dry leaves from a rubber plant.

The curled, dry leaves of the rubber plant suggested a large "Curled Leaves" hanging to Laurie Funk. The dead leaves had real sculptural quality. Without trying to copy a leaf, Laurie set out to explore whether twined jute might naturally shape itself in a similarly sculptural way. The first leaf did have this quality so she twined many leaves, varying the sizes and the proportions.

Hanging
of twined strips
based on
New Zealand flax.

New Zealand flax leaves.

same thing happens when strips are twined over stiff jute warps. Compare the photograph of flax leaves with the detail of Helen Dickey's hanging. It shows how further variation was achieved in the length of the strips and in the color tones of the yarn. The colors range from gold to golden-green.

Barnacles, the way they group themselves on anything to which they can attach, the shape of each individual form, the delicacy of the color, in fact everything about them is of

Barnacles.

interest to Rae Kipf. The obvious way to transform them into
fiber art is to repeat and group them on a background, repetition with variation.

The background Rae selected is soft purple in color.
She twined this in an oval shape since curves seem to belong
to the sea. Each barnacle shape was twined separately out of
handspun yarn especially dyed to suggest light sea green and
mauve. She arranged and rearranged the separate shapes and
let all of our group have a turn at it. The repeated shapes
which vary in color tone and in size were then attached to the
background.

Barnacles were interpreted by Valerie Bechtol in different
materials but still by repetition with variation. She attached
canvas to a large hoop and applied washes of paint in light

tones of sea green. The cylinders representing the barnacles are attached at right angles to the background. Each one hides a small mirror which reflects a good deal of light. Strands of silky, unknotted fiber in tones of green unify the composition.

Wall hanging by Rae Kipf.

Another interpretation of barnacles by Valerie Bechtol.

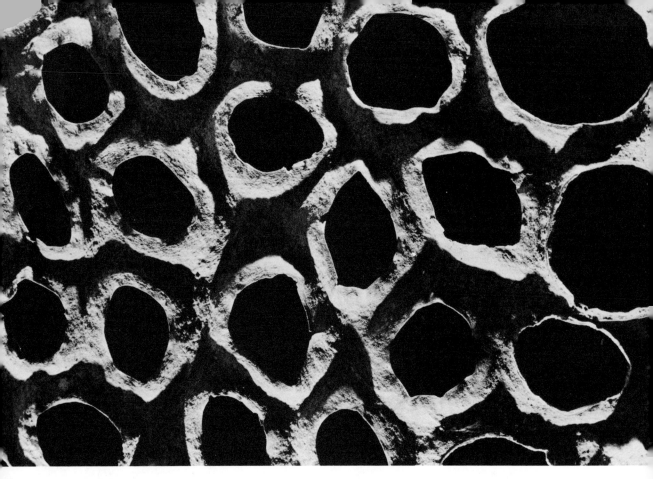

Seedpods of
the water lily.

Almost everyone knows the shape of the leaves of a water
lily, the flat surface that lies on top of the water and on which
frogs are supposed to sit. Not so familiar is the seedpod.
These are shaped like a ballerina's frilly skirt, a skirt turned
upside down since the "waist" of the skirt attaches to the
stem. The top of each bell shape is perforated with interesting
holes beneath which the seeds are nestled. I have spent many
hours studying the variation in the repeated holes. Some are
almost round but others are five-sided. Almost every one has
little dents and irregularities. It seemed that a stitchery
would be a good medium to interpret these variations. I
selected an orange linen background over which to layer
theatrical gauze in a paler orange, a gold, and a beige.

The first step in developing this design was to cut several dark shapes, each one a different size and slightly different in contour. These were freely cut out of black construction paper and arranged in various ways on newspaper until one way seemed satisfying. The next step was to decide upon the size of the panel. The area occupied by the dark shapes determined this roughly, and after looking for a while at the shapes resting on the paper, the exact dimensions were decided upon. The third step was to "frame" each dark area. Perhaps this occurred to me because each dark shape represented, in the beginning, a hole in the seedpod. The "framing" gave me a reason to use another color tone of fabric and I wanted this overlay because gauze is partly transparent.

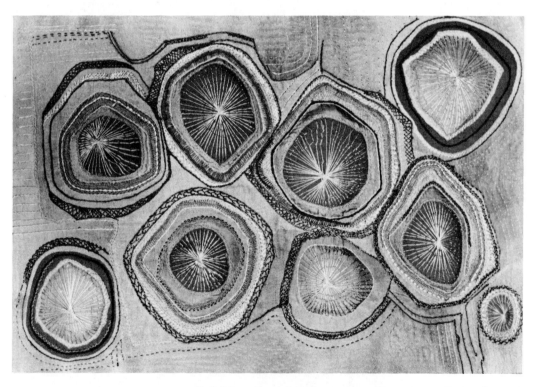

Stitching developed from water lily pads, by Esther Dendel.

When layers are stacked up and can be seen through, a feeling of rich depths takes place.

Using
Part of a Form
and
Building on It

A green pepper was the subject of Cynthia Hickok's investigation. She prepared herself to work by emptying her mind of all other things, accepting for the time being only its presence, the color, the shape, the odor, filling her world.

Green pepper sliced in half.

First, it was cut in half. She observed how the wall tapered from thin to thick, and the patterned clusters of seeds. A delicious peppery smell emanated from the cut flesh. The waxy green outside skin was the color of new grass. This pepper offered too many ideas for a single stitchery. To eliminate some of them, Cynthia put the green color out of her mind and narrowed her observation to just one section. To assist in this, she made a little cardboard frame. By looking through the opening or "window" in this, she selected the section she wished to study. The broken lines in her drawing indicate the area.

Drawing of pepper and
selection of the part to use.

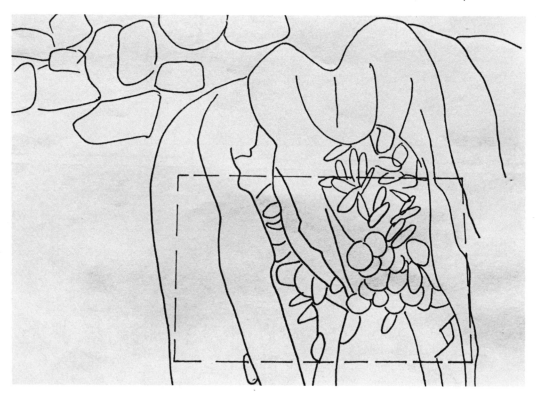

The next step was to view her drawing, not as a pepper, but as a design which started with a fully sensed pepper. Some lines were straightened, some were bent to keep the composition from sliding out of the picture area in the lower right. The seeds became circular shapes. She felt these needed repeating outside the original shape so she added some at the right side.

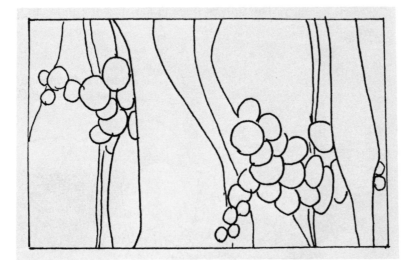

Balancing the design with changed lines and added seeds.

Planning the values of the colors for the stitching.

The finished panel.

After working on the design to her satisfaction, she was ready to decide on colors and textures. The green color seemed too overwhelming, so she switched to beiges, browns, and rusts. The lightest areas are the background. Each succeeding color tone is increasingly padded so the darkest areas stand out considerably from the background. The circles are also padded. Some lines are textured yarns couched on the surface. The scribbles in the drawing are crocheted areas, applied to the surface and stretched. The size is 29 inches by 40 inches.

In these pictures you can trace the evolution of the design idea. Now it is no longer a pepper, no longer green, but a statement in its own right.

Enlarging
a Single Form

A single form, a bone, an ear of corn, a leaf, an apple, in fact almost anything takes on significance when it is isolated from its fellows and enlarged. This is an effective design device.

Corn has special meaning to people who grew up on a Midwestern farm. Indeed, plump kernels on well-filled ears

Ear of corn.

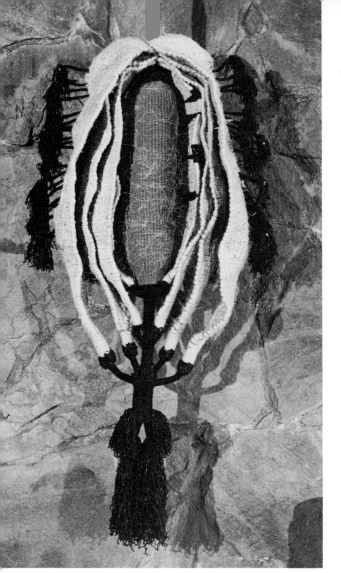

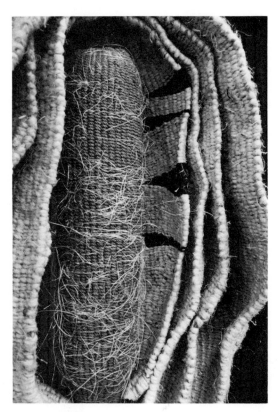

Corn sculpture.

Unspun sisal is used with red seine cord in center section.

and bursting bins meant the difference between privation and having enough income to get through the year. These early experiences linger in the back of the mind. A large ear of corn is a symbol of plenty as well as a beautiful sculptural form. The overall dimension of Jo Dendel's twined corn is 23 inches by 55 inches. Seine cord was used for the ear and jute for the husks. The tasseled bottom suggests, but does not imitate, the short bracing roots which support the stalk.

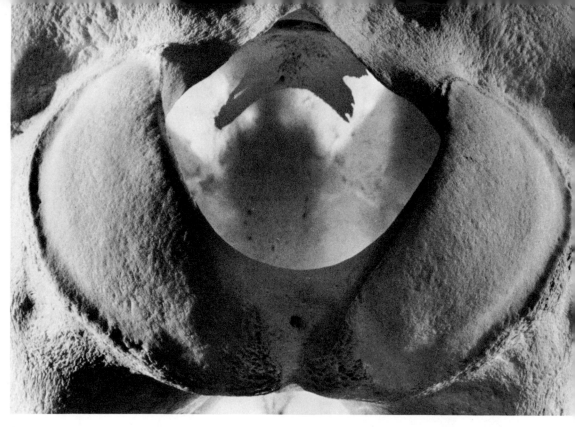

Sea lion bone.

Bone-inspired weaving.

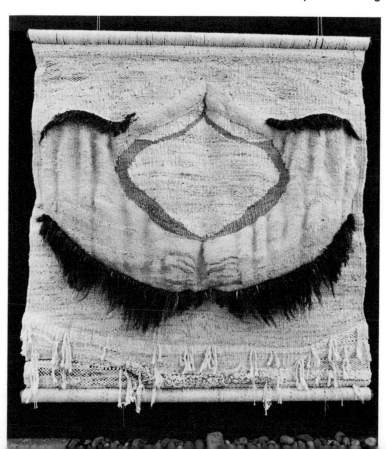

The study of a tiny fragment of bleached bone from a sea lion started Doris Fox on a large weaving, 5 feet by 5 feet. The shape of the curved portion of the bone was cut out of muslin in the designing stage. Two sizes were cut so they could be pinned on the warp and studied. The small one overlapped the large one in a pleasant way so it was decided to use both shapes. A double set of warps was used in order to be able to pad the raised areas.

Eucalyptus seeds are intriguing shapes with real sculptural quality. After studying a single seedpod, Laurie Funk twined a pod in jute, large enough for a table sculpture.

Eucalyptus pod
table sculpture.

Burned section of telephone pole.

Thinking in Shapes   One can develop an effective design simply by deciding to think shape. The section of a burned telephone pole caught our eye because the charred areas tend to be squares and rectangles, shapes which are not easily found in natural objects. The vertical fissures in the wood divide the pole into unequal segments. When Louella Ballerino pondered this, she visualized a weaving in which vertical stripes of a darker tone would make space divisions on which to superimpose rectangles which are also in the darker value. Had she not used the

"Thinking vertically" and "thinking square."
Woven and twined hanging based on charred telephone pole.

dark in the background weaving, the applied rectangles would have seemed "stuck on" instead of a part of the total statement.

To get the "feel" of thinking shape, it is helpful to sit down with a felt-tip pen to see how many variations of a single shape one can make into a composition. Sometimes Karen Page makes borders for her stationery with this kind of an exercise. I can never throw one of Karen's letters away because every page is a visual delight. The design shown here suggests some of the variations that can be made simply by "thinking square."

If you are more comfortable with curves, try "thinking round." Or, "think egg." For some other "thinks," try "tall" or "squat."

"Thinking square." Design with felt-tip pen.

"Thinking Sea Shapes."

Working without any particular object before her but simply by "thinking sea shapes," Judith Whelan was able to develop a textural weaving which she mounted on suede leather of a soft blue color. The hanging speaks of the sea and its creatures without being specific about any one species.

Design by Abstracting

An abstract is the concentrated essence of a larger whole. One takes away what is not essential to the understanding of a form. No distracting detail obscures what remains. All the qualities which do not help define the form have been eliminated.

Let us think of a fox. If I draw a line which suggests fluid motion, that is indeed characteristic of a fox. But it is also typical of much of the animal world so that line alone does not "say" fox. I think of the bushy tail, a great beautiful brush. The face is essentially a triangle. The ears are small, triangular, and alert. The color is rusty red. Combining these characteristics adds up to the essential form of a fox.

Now let us look at a frog. I think of large, round, protruding eyes. The head is shaped rather like a slice of melon turned upside down. The mouth is petulant and large enough to emit a startling croak. The arms are rather puny compared to the powerful legs. I assign Mr. Frog the personality of a somewhat bored but aggressive and watchful chairman of the board presiding over a meeting of stockholders.

Which of the three frogs, all of them by Jean Hudson, best represents the quintessence of frog? If the round format seems more suitable for presenting a frog, why is this true? Does the patterning of one of the forms detract from its

Frog #1.

"froginess" or enhance it? If you close the book, which of the frogs can you recall most exactly? In which frog is the power of the hind legs best suggested?

Frog #2.

Frog #3.

In designing by abstraction, it is necessary to give thought to the relative importance of each shape. This is valuable experience. It helps sharpen our observation and it gives us a sensitivity to natural forms of all kinds. As an exercise, try drawing a familiar creature after writing a description of the salient features, their shape and size. When you have finished, look at the animal or at a photograph of one. Have you caught him through your observation and understanding? If not, keep on trying. People often decide, quite erroneously, that they cannot draw after making one or two feeble attempts. Being able to draw does not make one an artist, but the ability helps you make your statement.

Search for Meanings

Rust,
Termites, and
Tension

Rust, termites, and tension. The words recall Biblical references to "rust and moths consumeth." We must look again. It is only when a discarded piece of plumbing is so rusted and weathered that it no longer is seen as plumbing that it takes on a different beauty as a new and different entity. It dies as a lavatory to be resurrected as abstract sculpture. Classification imprisons objects in a category; declassification liberates them. Only by becoming trash do they become available to be something else. When we divorce a utilitarian object from its utility and bring it into a new setting to enjoy its color or shape or texture or patina, we have reclassified it. It has become junk art.

I have a doll made by a Turkana man for his daughter. Among the many strings of beads which encircle its neck is half of a broken zipper. Because it is broken and has no utility as a closing device, it has attained a new status. One may say that it has been declassified as a zipper and reclassified as a serrated circle. Africans have great talent for this. Tourists who smile because a Masai has used an old beer can for an earplug do not understand this aspect of art.

One may look into a can of old nails. Some are bent. Some have heads that were deformed long ago while they were being relieved of their holding function (utility). All are

99

flaking rust. When we take them out of the can and begin to arrange them in various ways, they become design units. They have already been declassified as nails.

It takes a certain maturity of mind to accept that nature works as steadily in rust as in rose petals. If one is to make something inspired by these found objects, it is necessary to go beyond arrangement. One could learn as much about design by arranging shiny new pins on a black cardboard. Few meanings attach to new pins.

Because it is an earthy fiber and in no way showy or elegant, Doris Fox used jute to make her interpretation of rusty nails. We can call the knob at the end of each unit a head, but it is no longer a nail head. It is a design element, a *dot* or

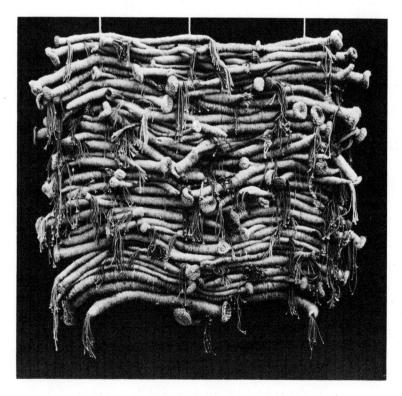

Nail wall hanging of twined and wrapped natural jute with accents of red seine cord.

Detail of
the nail hanging.

spot. A period. The body of each nail has become a tapered *shape.* The dominant *direction* is parallel but with deviation for interest. The heads or dots are sometimes red instead of natural jute color in order to lead the eye through the composition. This is design thinking.

What, then, about meanings? Each artist expresses his own. Why did the can of rusty nails attract Doris in the first place? Her mind went back to her pioneer ancestors who desperately needed this scarce item to build shelters. She thought of square nails made, one by one and by hand, which are still holding together a few houses in Middle America. Old nails as well as barbed wire are symbols of the frontier. One can look into a can of old nails and see an entire panorama of the expansion of the West.

Someone else might see a different symbolism. Nails hold things together. They connect things which would otherwise be separate. All artists and other people, too, are interested in connection. Alienated persons are lacking connectedness. One thinks of one's own sturdy connections. This manner of thinking leads to a rich inner life. One owes it to oneself to have interesting thoughts.

The finished piece is not just something to "pretty" a room. It is well designed and it holds hidden significance. When we find our own symbolism in it, we are participating in it. We are then a part of what has been done.

TERMITES

A little way outside the town of Oshogbo in Nigeria is a forest sacred to the river goddess, Oshun. It is enclosed by a beautiful, undulating fence made of mud coated with cement. In the Yoruba language the words for worshiping a god also mean to make a god. Many gods have been made of mud and set in little shrines among the fallen leaves of the forest.

One enters this grove through a magnificent sculptured entrance which has a thatch roof above it to protect the mud from which it is made. Passing into and through the sculpture is an overwhelming experience. One must stoop and bow down to negotiate the passages which suggest to a sensitive pilgrim the mysteries of birth. One enters as a citizen of the modern world and emerges as a child of Mother Earth. These, at least, were my emotions.

This awe-inspiring entrance was created by an unschooled bricklayer turned sculptor, Adebisi Akanji. He was helped and inspired by a remarkable European artist, Susanne Wenger, who went to Nigeria in 1950. She found that the beliefs of the Yoruba people held universal truths. Her understanding of these was so deep and sympathetic that they trusted her with the repair of their most sacred shrines.

Inside the silent grove, one walks slowly, careful not to stumble over the many termite mounds and molded sculptured shrines. One must look closely to tell whether some of these are man-made art that has weathered or the product of termite sculpture. Not only in this forest but throughout Africa, termites have worked the soil into new formations. In Liberia we made houses out of the soil that had passed through their tiny bodies, using it to plaster walls because it made a better plaster than ordinary mud. Termites have a bad name with us, but they are the original and industrious recyclers of cellulose. Their constructions fascinate me as much as man-made sculptures. Sometimes they rework a bamboo fence, doing their own plastering to form protective tunnels. Sometimes their industry patterns the outside of a log.

A study of the log shows that the pattern is essentially a maze. There is an unexplainable fascination about a maze. Books for children present them as entertaining puzzles to be worked. Our unconscious aesthetic responses are often caught in myths and legends. You will remember that Theseus went boldly into the labyrinth to slay the Minotaur with a sword in his hand and a skein of thread which Ariadne had thoughtfully provided to enable him to find his way out. The author must have been as intrigued with passages that turn and twist and lead into one another as we are. Does not life confront us all with paths that run into dead ends and with an assortment of Minotaurs to slay? Theseus was victorious not only because he had courage, but also because he was equipped with a sword and an unbroken thread. And something more. He had Ariadne's love.

The possibilities for finding personal symbolism in this are endless. In my own life I see the unbroken thread unwinding with the passing years as not only my own past but

Termite patterns on a log.

After studying the termite-patterned log, Jo Granger worked a similar pattern in appliqué on the front of a blouse.

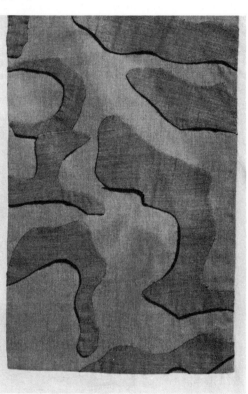

the past of my parents, and their parents, going back to Europe and to ancestors of whom I have no knowledge. This is my karma. My sword is whatever wisdom I have acquired to meet problems as they arise. As to the Minotaurs in my life, I will not go into that here. You have your own to think about.

One is free to add one's own workings to those of the termites' patterning. That is what Jean Stange has done in a
pillow top she appliquéd and quilted. Starting with a tracing

First step in developing design from a termite maze.

on tissue paper of the termite maze, she thickened some of the shapes, bent some of the lines, and gave the composition a central point of interest. We can follow the successive steps of her designing from the sketches she made.

Second step in design.

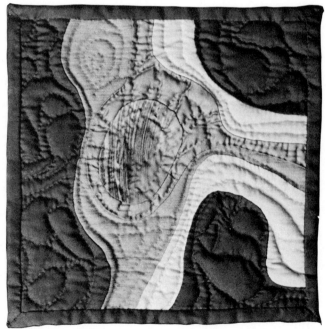

The finished appliquéd and
quilted pillow top.

TENSION

The pattern of cracked mud is formed by surface tension as sun and wind dry the earth's moist skin. Tension has a bad name in our culture but in actual fact even a jellyfish would disintegrate without the cohesive force of tension. What people try to get rid of with everything from aspirin to Yoga and Zen is unproductive tension, stresses which tighten muscles and block the flow of feeling and nourishing blood.

Creative tension, and I believe there is no creation without tension, is built up in the body and mind and then pleasurably released by the rhythmic act of making, whether the thing made is a poem, a painting, a pot, or a new kind of pancake. Tension is a tremendous source of energy. It is only when it is not discharged in rhythmic action that it comes out as a headache. Johannes Itten, who taught the basic course in design at the famous Bauhaus, had his students do rhythmic exercises before they started to draw. He wanted the act of drawing to start at the toes and flow through the entire body. Work and rest, inhaling and exhaling, the concentrated mind and the emptying of all thought, day and night, ebb and flow, we need the entire cycle, not just half of it. We all know people who seem to bend all their energies toward getting relaxed. If they would get into the swing of exciting, creative work, they would get relaxed without even thinking about it. Some take sedatives. They have opted for the jellyfish. If they were to put everything they had into throwing pots or making a garden, or beating weft, and did it with feeling and with the entire body, how different their lives might become. No more chemical sedatives.

When the glaze on a piece of pottery does not expand and contract with the same rhythm as the clay body, the unwanted tension which results is called crazing. When crazing is con-

Cracked, dried mud.

Peeling paint.

trolled and desired, it is called crackle. It is at its most beautiful in ancient Chinese porcelains. Crazing is "bad" tension, crackle is "good" tension. So it is in life. The choice is between creative tension discharged in pleasure and destructive tension which is difficult to discharge in any way. Craftsmen are lucky because it is the nature of their work to provide the kind of tension in which every muscle and nerve contribute to good feeling.

When paint peels from a building, it is "bad" as far as the preservation of the building is concerned, but it may be very productive, "good" tension for the artist who studies it. Contemplating the curls of detached pigment, noting what paint does when it is free to follow its innate nature, one begins to see the disintegrating surface as far more interesting than it ever could have been in its pristine freshness. It has peeled for the same reason that glaze crazes, the surface and the body expand and contract in different rhythms.

After studying some rather spectacular spirals made by several layers and colors of almost detached paint, I decided to experiment with twined jute. In twining, the bottom ends of the warp hang free and are not compelled to stay rigid as in the case with warp on a loom. The back layer of my hanging is rust-colored wool. The front layer of jute is twined in ribbon-like, narrow strips. Jute does not curl in the same way as loose paint, but the patterns formed are similar.

Hanging based on peeling paint.

In the unspoiled little village of Dodowa in Ghana, we watched the women making beautiful pots. As an unexpected bonus we noted the way the whitewash was peeling off the mud huts, making exciting patterns in dark and light. The villagers laughed as we moved about discussing the patterns and taking pictures. Julia George transformed parts of these patterns into batiks. They take us back to a place we love and are eloquent of their source.

Batik by Julia George. Design developed from studying patterns of peeled whitewash in an African village.

Tension lines in a Masai house wall
in Serengeti, Kenya.

The Masai people of East Africa make their houses by plastering a framework of sticks with cow dung. As the dung dries, it shrinks, and the resulting patterns are incredibly beautiful. The designs formed are an almost flower-like mosaic with exposed portions of the stick framework suggesting stems. The Masai love their cows with a passion which an outsider cannot comprehend. Even the excreta has

"Cowslip," a tapestry developed from a study of the Masai house wall.

an almost mystic attraction for them. Their attitude calls into question our own revulsion toward body waste.

The small weaving suggested to me by the Masai house I have called "Cowslip" because the original Middle English name of that little flower was *cowslyppe*, meaning cow dung or cow paste. The flower is an Old World primrose whose Latin name is *Primula veris*.

When our bottle of antacid went down suddenly, I became apprehensive about my husband's health until he showed me what he had been doing with it. Spread out in his studio were various containers containing dried and cracked antacid. Different kinds of patterns developed according to the thickness of the coating. A thin-to-thick layer produces a small-to-large pattern.

Antacid tension pattern.
A thin-to-thick layer sets up a small-to-large progression of shapes.

A coating of antacid on a curved dish assumes different shapes and makes a dramatic pattern.

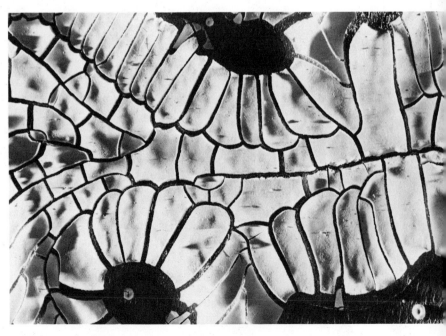

Antacid tension creating negative shapes.

In some cases the antacid tension was sufficient to pull the coating entirely away from areas, creating negative shapes. Lois Martin interpreted this pattern of stress and strain in a padded batik for a pillow.

The padded batik.

It may come as a surprise to learn that stress is a stimulus to growth. D'Arcy Thompson tells us that weighting the stalk of a pear while the pear is growing and ripening increases the strength remarkably without causing any increase in bulk. He also points out that taffy is easily stretched and pulled when one begins to work it. With each doubling back on itself and restretching, the mass becomes stronger and more difficult to work because the molecules have rearranged themselves.

Kneading bread dough works toward a similar rearrangement and increased strength. Those of us who spin fleece have seen how the stress of twisting it produces a strong cord. Thompson points out that the danger of breakdown or rupture in metal under stress is lessened the more that the materials are arranged along the tension lines of the system. When we comb our hair, the hairs which lie in the path of the comb's progress are not disturbed, but those lying obliquely to the comb's direction are "brought into the tension lines of the system." Does it not seem worthwhile to meditate upon what things in one's life are awry and what areas need rearrangement? How are we to bring certain distracting odds and ends, the wild hairs, into the direction of the comb? What stresses induce growth and enable us to fulfill our potential? For myself, I know that if I don't have a deadline, I had better give myself one.

Having a purpose in life and being under sufficient stress to implement accomplishing it lead to a quickened pace, a bright eye, a feeling of health and strength. Sometimes when people are suddenly relieved of the stress of having to make a living, their lives become rudderless and unhappy. They may "take up a hobby" but it holds no meaning. There is no emotional charge in making something in a mechanical way.

No one can just fiddle around with a project in a perfunctory manner when he has nothing better to do and expect to get any good out of it. Forming without feeling is a time filler or a time killer. Emerson told us what we need to do. We need, he said, the power to "swell the moment from the resources of the heart." The ability to do this depends upon the way we turn experience into readiness for action. And readiness for action means placing ourselves under creative tension.

Wood,
Roots, and
Growth

"Whenever you think, or you believe, or you know, you're a lot of other people, but the moment you *feel*, you are nobody but yourself." I wish I knew who said that because I think it expresses an important truth. What we are seeking in our craft work is growth through complete, tranced involvement. We try to enter into the experience of making something as though we were entering the interior of a whole new world, being enclosed and absorbed in it.

When this is achieved, it is an altered state of consciousness. It is a rare experience to feel oneself *within* something or someone who ordinarily is *other*. These are peak experiences.

Almost everyone has had a few peak experiences which are so far out of the ordinary that the memory of them lingers for years. It is only recently that one dares to speak freely and without embarrassment of changed states of consciousness. These are ecstatic experiences during which one sees familiar objects in a way they are not usually seen. One such experience has nourished me during all the years since it happened. When I recall it, there is always the question, "Why can we not see things in this intense way at any time, at will?"

I was in college and very hungry. Many of the ecstatic visions the saints have described have happened after they fasted. This may indicate that these experiences do not happen with a full stomach. However, one may fast without any expansion of perception. One cannot will a peak experience into being. It arrives as a sort of grace. The setting was an art laboratory where skeins of yarn were stored in a bank of drawers beneath windows. As I opened one of these drawers, the sun was streaming through the windows and struck directly on the yarn.

Suddenly, it seemed to me that the source of light was

within the yarns. The reds appeared as ruby and hot as embers. I was afraid to touch them. They would have seared my hands. The oranges pulsed like stars. And the golds were like a soft fallout of fireworks, slow, deliberate, rich. All of the strands seemed translucent and they trembled with the intensity of light they seemed to be giving out. They were alive, breathingly alive.

There is no way of knowing how long I stood there entranced, because time had ceased to exist. I know that the teacher came eventually, closed the drawer, and asked me if anything was wrong.

To this day, I thrill to golds and oranges and reds but never again have I seen them quite as I saw them then. Many times since I have had lesser peak experiences. Once a bare sycamore tree, hung with seedpods like festival lanterns, glowed against the sky. Each branch, each twig, each pod was outlined with a pale gold aura. I felt the surge of sap in my own veins, the pull of moisture through the roots embedded in black, fecund loam. I seemed enveloped in a throbbing vitality which enclosed myself and the tree in a transparent bubble of golden energy.

Perhaps if these transfigured moments came too often, we could not bear their intensity. What they do for us is to point up the way things look when we are seeing them at the height of perception.

We read in Frazer's *Golden Bough,* "To the savage, the world in general is animate, and trees and plants are no exception to the rule." I believe exactly that and I do not consider myself a savage.

In the time of Caesar, the Germans whom he questioned about their homeland said that it was possible to travel through dense forest for two months without coming to the ends of the trees. Much of the forest was without paths. Anyone who dared to deface the bark of a living tree was subject to dreadful penalties under the old German laws. Only three generations separate my brother and myself from the forests of Germany and the Germans age-old veneration of trees. In my own childhood in Iowa, a maypole was set up in the schoolyard and we wove a bright wrapping for it as we danced with streamers of colored paper. I don't believe anyone told us that this custom came directly from the days when tree worship was common in much of Europe.

From the time I could read Hans Christian Andersen and the Brothers Grimm, I knew that dryads live in hollow trees, that I could go to visit them and trust them with my deepest secrets. There was a hollow tree in our pasture where my favorite dryad lived and I used to take her candy in the pocket of my apron. When I went to live in Africa, it did not seem in any way strange that people left offerings among the buttress roots of the great silk-cotton trees. When I saw my first baobab tree, I felt that its great hollow trunk must be a tube running deep into time, a tunnel that led back to the days before men walked the vast and ancient continent.

Dryads no longer converse with me except in an oft-recurring dream in which I exchange places with one for a time, and while I am tree-bound, I feel the breeze combing my hair and the feet of little birds tickling my scalp in a delightful way. With forests and trees looming so importantly in my racial heritage and in my childhood, it is only natural that I find much food for feeling in contact with wood and roots. I know that growth is a pulling in and a stretching and a giving out. The roots have to go deeper before the shoots can grow taller. When I study a tree, I like to imagine the mirror image of its form below the surface in the damp earth.

The biography of a burned and weathered plank is written on its surface. As we study it, we find it easy to imagine that the almost-human shapes we see are wood spirits released by fire. The charred areas are purple in their depths and many tones of gray on the surface. There is a sort of fairy-tale magic before us. This suggested a shadow-box weaving to Bulu Rollyson who placed the figures on the back level. We look through an irregular opening in the front to discover them.

If you have read C. S. Lewis's wonderful books, *The Chronicles of Narnia,* you will remember that Lucy stepped into a wardrobe, and after feeling her way through the fur coats she reached the back which opened out into the magic land of Narnia. Alice had to disappear from the surface world through a rabbit hole. Bulu's figures have to be reached through the window she has opened for us. Delightful as this weaving is, its greatest value is the quality of thought which is possible if one has not outgrown the capacity for fantasy. What other creatures people the shadowy paths through the woods behind the two we are able to see? One of the things we need most in America is dream time, time for waking dreams, time for fantasy.

We have not said much about technique in this book because the right technique will be discovered if the concept is strong. Technique is invented out of the need to express something. The warp for this piece was wrapped around and around a two-inch-wide frame made of weathered wood. The wood had to be weathered and the weaving had to be in two separated layers because of what it says.

The manner in which a wounded tree heals itself has obvious lessons for all of us. The scars remain, scars perhaps of a broken friendship, a lost spouse, a deep disappointment.

Burned plank.

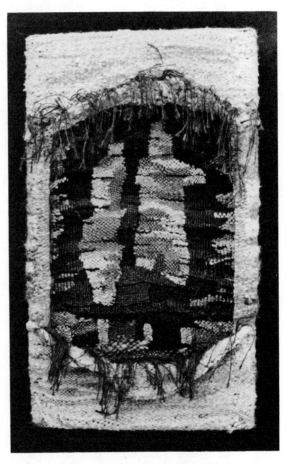

"Wood Spirits" by Bulu Rollyson.

Healed wound on a tree.

Growth continues, the tree survives. A special kind of growth encloses and forms a protective ridge around the wounded area.

You may look at Charla Rudolph's weaving without any thought of a tree trunk. You would see a textural, two-layered hanging with an irregular opening in the center front, through which you see a smoother, golden layer beneath. You might find some symbolism in it which has nothing to do with a tree. Or you might simply enjoy its color and texture. That is as it should be. The meanings in our work are not inherent in the work but in the maker or the viewer. And the viewer is free to supply his own.

Weaving based on the scarred tree trunk.

Mixed in with the jute and the yarn in **Charla Rudolph's** weaving are strips cut from a worn sweater of her husband's. The ends of these are allowed to hang free and frankly declare their history as a garment.

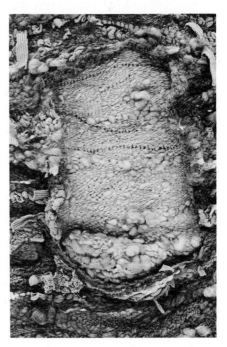

Weaving in
burnt orange jute with
unspun sisal and wrapped
cords by Ann Dryer.

Even without a dryad in residence, a hollow tree can be
the residence of all kinds of creatures—rodents, beetles,
bees, coons, "stump water," and all the minute life stagnate
water supports. A hollow tree we saw in Angers, France,
seemed as ancient and mysterious as the walled citadel we
had come to admire. The weaving which Ann Dryer did when
she was back home has wrapped cords in surprise colors
within to symbolize the mysterious life which thrives in the
dark shelter of the hollow trunk.

In East Africa the bark of the fever tree splits in deep
fissures. It has the appearance of growing so fast that it
splits its skin. Where the outer bark has been worn off, perhaps by an elephant rubbing his back against it, delicate
traceries of the outer pattern remain. As a further texture,

Fever tree bark.

brilliant lichens often grow in clusters over the entire trunk. Jim and Pat Wood wove their interpretation of the fever tree using flat and tufted areas. They made it for a rug but we persuaded them to hang it on the wall.

Fever tree bark weaving for a wall rug.

The craft work we do with our hands gives evidence to ourselves and others of the visible growth we are making above the surface in the light and air. Meanwhile our roots are probing deeper and wider in darkness and silence. This, perhaps is the more important growth. It is the dark and hidden side that nourishes the plant with nutrient-laden moisture. There are rocks beneath the surface. Our roots find detours around them. I have seen fairly large boulders completely em-

Tree roots around a boulder in Jos, Nigeria.

braced and held by a tangle of roots wrapped about them. Usually the tree has to be uprooted before this can be seen. But in the northern Nigerian town of Jos, there is a tree which has coped in a rather spectacular way with the rocky landscape in which it grows. I look at the photograph and rejoice that roots are not stopped by rocks that happen to be in the way. I shall weave this into a tapestry someday after I have had more time to think about it.

Bones, Magic, and the Unconscious

A contemporary trend, especially in the fabric arts, is the widespread use of articles which might well have been pulled out of an African shaman's medicine pouch. Bones and teeth, animal horn, fur and feathers, have the pull and power in the unconscious of talismanic pieces endowed with magic. It may be that we are nostalgic for an age when belief came easier. Lacking magic in our daily lives, must we try to invoke it with rabbit pelts and pheasant skins hung in our weavings?

During the Middle Ages a sense of magic blended with religion when the cult of relics caused great cathedrals to be built to house a scrap of cloth or a holy bone. Thousands of pilgrims walked the hazardous nine hundred miles from Paris to Santiago de Compostela in Spain because the bones of St. James were thought to rest there. In the legendary battle of Clavijo in 844, the vastly outnumbered Christians saw the figure of St. James riding a white horse before them, swinging a great sword and leading them to victory.

Those Christians sorely needed the help of St. James because the Moors kept an arm of the Prophet in a vault in Córdoba. They carried the arm with them when they went into battle and firmly believed themselves to be invincible because of their holy relic.

I mention these instances of reverence for bones, not to scoff at them, but to point out that from ancient times down to the present day bones have held a special place in our emotional life. This is part of our heritage.

Leaving fantasy and magic aside for a moment and taking a cool, scientific look at living bone with the eye of an engineer, it is difficult to imagine a more perfect structure. Our bones are constructed to deal with stresses and strains due both to compression and tension. One need not be an engineer to see that the form of a bone is extremely beautiful. Our great American painter, Georgia O'Keeffe, remembers gathering up a barrel of bones on our Western desert and sending them back to her studio in New York. Her paintings of bleached skulls and vertebrae have taught us to appreciate the stark beauty of bare bones.

William Butler Yeats wrote a poem called "The Collar Bone of a Hare," in which he finds the bone worn thin by the lapping of water and pierces it with a gimlet in order to stare through the hole at the "old bitter world" through "the white thin bone of a hare." With this simple imagery, he is telling us something profound.

A physician friend who has a touch of the poet in him tells me that he sees living bones as beautiful and mysterious caverns in whose caves the lifeblood of man is manufactured. To many of our workshop group who have thought about bones as a design source, they symbolize character, that most enduring part of ourselves. They are an armature of strength in the midst of flux. We could not stand on our two feet either physically or morally without them.

Each of us can learn a great deal about ourself by noting

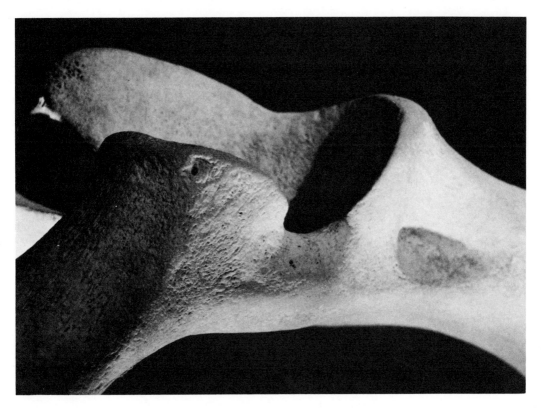

Bleached bone.

the way in which we respond to bones, or to any other natural structure. Psychologists of the Jungian school of thought have pointed out that we have four ways of functioning. These are thinking, feeling, sensation, and intuition.

Thinking analyzes. The engineer who sees that the lines of stress in a bone or in a bridge run at a certain angle to one another is analyzing. In our culture there is great emphasis and financial reward for this manner of functioning. We are under the tyranny of a society which often seems to value only this one capacity. I think we need to be chary of too much analyzing. We can all too easily pull all the petals off the daisy and have nothing left but a denuded stem.

Feeling is sometimes confused with intuition. A chief difference according to the Jungians is that feeling is a rational process, while intuition is not. Feeling evaluates. If I ask your opinion about a certain design, I am asking you to make a "good" or a "bad" judgment of it, not to reason why.

Sensation is a way of perceiving. Much of this book is about visual and other sensory perception. It does not judge, it simply receives. In most of us it is a function which needs to be sharpened.

Intuition enables us to perceive inner meanings. I do not believe that intuition can be taught. It can be fostered. It can manifest itself as a sudden flash which comes from we know not where. Silence and rest help make this possible.

It is imperative that each of our four functions be strong if we are to become well-rounded persons. In almost everyone, one of the four is dominant. The weakest is likely to be apparent to one's friends, if not to oneself. How does one nurture the weak function? It has been suggested by Irene de Casillejo, who wrote *Knowing Woman*, that the way to do this is to pour less energy into the stronger ones. If I am too busy thinking, the intuitive side of my nature goes dormant. I can aim for less mental activity and for more silence within. If I am to become the creative person I want to be, I must rearrange my life so this is possible.

Suppose that when Archimedes stepped into his now famous bath, he had been pondering how to get the tub retiled. (Logical thinking.) Or suppose he had been deciding to reject a tiled tub, considering them a "bad" surface, and was about to have his gardener dig a natural-looking pool in the garden giving him a "good" place for his ablutions? (Feeling.) Or what if he had responded only to the smoothing lapping of warm water about his limbs? (Sensation.) He must have been doing none of these because suddenly his attention focused on something he already must have seen many times without attaching any significance to it. The water level rose in the tub as his body was lowered into it. In a flash, which is the way of intuitions, he realized that the amount by which the water level was raised corresponded to the volume of his body which was immersed.

Now Archimedes had been working with his rational mind on a problem he had not been able to solve by thinking about it. He had been asked to evaluate whether a crown owned by Hiero of Syracuse was pure gold or had been adulterated with a cheaper metal. Had he been able to melt down the complicated crown and make it into a bar whose volume he could measure and weigh, he could have solved the problem with his thinking function because he knew the specific weight of gold. But how to measure the volume of a crown ornamented with complicated filigree? As he relaxed in his bath, his unconscious offered the solution.

In my own experience, intuition works after my thinking mind has been frustrated by failure to solve a difficulty in a rational way. We need the pressure of *specific* unsolved problems. Archimedes needed the problem of the crown as much as he needed the relaxation of his bath.

Intuition is a poetic function because it deals in analogies. I write poetry because finding hidden correspondences facilitates the functioning of my intuition which I value highly. Doing our necessary bookkeeping inhibits it. The energy I pour into my poetry helps restore the balance.

And where may we look to satisfy our longing for authentic magic? There are some truly great shamans in Africa whose powers are beyond dispute. I knew one of them. He seemed strangely careless about the bones and other gear in his medicine bag, although the people in the village feared to look at it, much less touch it. When I asked him about this, he

Bone study #1.

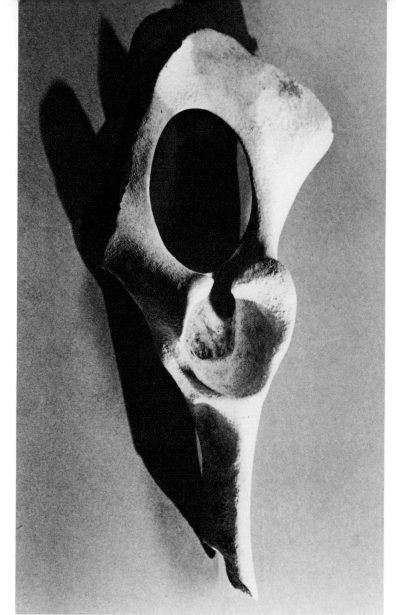

pointed to his chest in the region of his heart. "Power here," he said. Then pointing to the bag at his feet, "No power there."

To diagram the importance of each of the four functions in a well-balanced whole person, Jung drew a circle and labeled each fourth of the circumference for one of the functions. Since one makes what one is, it was in a spirit of self-discovery that our group studied and worked from bones. Which of the four functions would emerge as an individual's strongest? Which the weakest? The idea was not to duplicate or copy a particular bone but to use the bone as a starting point. The finished piece need not even resemble a bone. We

Beverly Kelly's sculptural form based on bone study #1. Seine cord was used for the warp and bleached jute for the twining.

The extent of development from the source is emphasized in this detail of Beverly Kelly's work.

A further study
by Beverly Kelly on
bone study #1.

recommend this way of working as a step toward greater knowledge of oneself.

What each person discovered about himself is of greatest interest to that individual, so we are presenting without comment some of the work that had its origin in our investigation

This tapestry by Jean Russom was based on bone study #1. Red and green yarns were used in the background to dramatize the white bone shape, which is woven and padded.

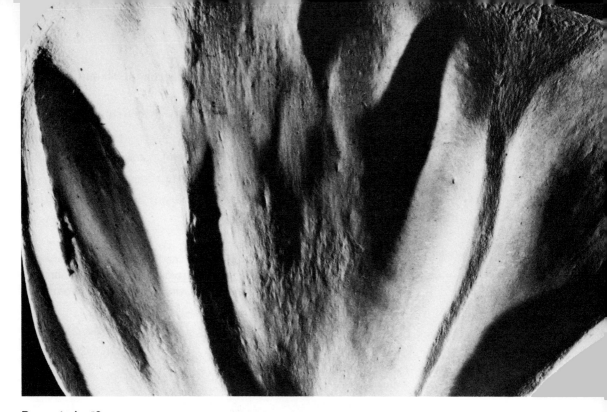

Bone study #2.

A hanging
by Ann Dryer for
bone study #2.

of bones. When ordinary objects are lighted by extraordinary attention, there is nothing spurious about the magic which happens.

Seeds, Seedpods, and Growth

When we were children on an Iowa farm, it was the custom to select the best ears of corn each fall and save them for the next year's seed. The ears were strung together in cradles of crossed twine so each part was exposed to the circulation of air. We had no separate room available for a seed room so it was necessary to hang these long strings of corn from the ceilings of our bedrooms. We objected to having our sleeping quarters so filled with grain that we could barely walk around the beds. This was not my idea of how a little girl's room should be decorated. If we got up in the dark (there was no electricity) and banged against one of the strings, it set up a fearful clatter as one heavy string of ears set the next one into motion. This aroused the whole household and there was considerable concern about whether any of the kernels had been chipped or bruised. It was presumed that small heads would mend but not damaged corn.

Our parents explained the necessity for the arrangement. They even tried to make us pleased about it. Each kernel was something much more than a dry, yellow grain. Each row on the ear was a row of green, growing corn in the field, leaves rippling in that special way peculiar to corn, and with good luck it would be "knee-high by the Fourth of July." At night when we sat on the well platform to escape the summer heat inside, we could hear a faint rustling in the corn when there was no breeze. Our mother said it was the sound of corn growing. It was growth music and we must be very still in order to hear it. My mother thought that corn fairies lived in the fields and that only children could hear their songs which are different from growth music. And sure enough, the great Carl Sandburg has confirmed this in his *Rootabaga Stories*. The corn fairies, he says, sit between the corn rows with their big toes pointing toward the moon and sew overalls out of corn leaves with corn silk. By keeping the seed corn in our rooms and away from mold, mildew, and rodents, we had the great privilege of being winter guardians of all this magic.

Even though we were not entirely convinced of our privileged status, we learned a great deal about imagination without the word having been mentioned. Imagination, among other things, is a way of making the present moment wonderful when, without it, the present would be barely tolerable. You can crack your head on the corn in the bitter cold and the dark. Or you can spin a little corn silk into the kind of thread the corn fairies need to sew their overalls. The choice is strictly up to you.

I am not always spinning silk; sometimes I am staggering in the dark. But it all comes down to this: If objects have no meaning in themselves but are only what we make them out to be, why not make them bright and gay and wonderful? Suppose I had been given a bedroom, cozy with central heating and a dressing table with pink ruffles? I would not be the person I now am. Part of me is snow on the window ledge and chilblains and spring thaw. Maybe the corn fairies charge admission to the corn rows. One banged head and one chilblain. Cheap at the price, and I wouldn't trade my ticket for all the central heating and electricity in the world. I rejoice that young people in increasing numbers are retreating to the land to plant gardens and grow along with their vegetables.

The biggest excitement of the long, cold winter was the arrival of seed catalogs with pictures of the most delectable fruits and vegetables ever imagined by man. Real rubies never glowed with the brilliance of the beets on those pages. The peas looked so juicy you almost expected to get squirted in the eye if you pressed a finger on the picture. I have never seen real blackberries as glossy and succulent as those in the catalog, but an American pioneer of still life named Raphael Peale knew how to paint them that way. I have always imagined that he painted his famous "Blackberries" in the middle of a severe winter. We had no fresh vegetables except for the root crops in the cellar after the first killing frost, so the promises in the seed catalog were like a vision of Paradise. Color photography had not been developed to its present high level at that time and I knew nothing of graphic processes, so I am still not certain how the radishes on the pages became so crimson or the lettuce so green. Now that frozen foods make it possible for us to have anything we want to eat at any time of the year, I wonder whether seed catalogs have lost their glow. Perhaps seeds are not the same to today's children, especially those who do not have a small garden to tend and plant. A child without a garden seems to me to be truly impoverished.

When we planted our garden in the spring, we left a marker in the row wherever an envelope of seed ran out and a new one started. The empty seed packet placed over the stake held out its bright promise until the seeds sprouted and grew. Each stake seemed to me like a little altar, a holy thing. To this day I cannot pass a rack filled with envelopes of seeds without pausing and feeling a little celebration, a welling up of gladness. A seed is not just a shape in nature's vast repertory; it is a symbol of hope, of eternity. It is seed that gives meaning to the flower. Seed force can lift a stone, break a wall, and crack the cement of your most ingrained

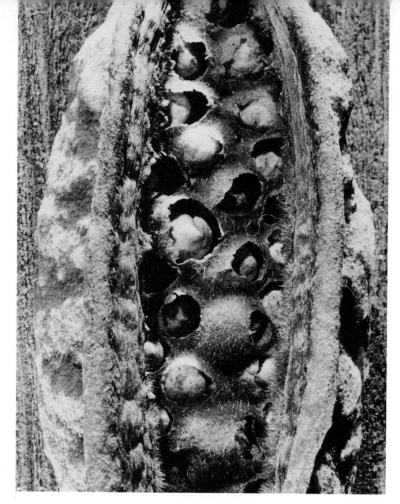

Seeds and seedpods of
the pink flame tree.

habit. It is time to get acquainted with the seed forces within
ourselves.

I have gone into some detail about the way I feel toward
seeds and seedpods because I believe it is important for each
of us to review old memories of things he has felt or done or
seen or heard or held. This personal emotional biography,
recalled and refelt, will help you get acquainted with the
child you once were and might help reawaken the sense of
wonder which comes naturally to children. A sense of wonder and a sense of the holiness of each humble thing are the
greatest of resources for a new kind of life, a new quality in
living.

Imagination is seeing an oak when you look at an acorn. Faith is *knowing* that that is the way it is. There is vitality in a person with faith. He walks with an air of expectation.

Our workshop group has shared their responses to seed and seed power. Many of the articles shown in this book which illustrate various other approaches to design had their origins in this sharing experience. Our seedpod collection is large and varied. A lovely one is the pod of the pink flame tree.

Bici Linklater interpreted this pod in a hanging in rust, gold, and mossy green.

White necklace with shells.

Use of Natural Materials

Incorporating Natural Materials with Fibers

The key to combining other natural materials with fibers lies in finding relationships. Too often they seem "stuck on" instead of belonging. Many good weavings are ruined by hanging them from a piece of driftwood just because the craftsman likes driftwood.

There are many possible relationships—line, color, scale, forms, and spirit of the work.

In a white necklace by Charla Rudolph, the added shells belong. One has to look closely to see that they are shells.

Necklace detail showing the larger shell.

145

They relate to the coiled and wrapped body of the work in color (white), in size, and in rhythmic statement. The rhythm in the largest shell is through *radiation*. That of the coiling is in *spiral movement*. The entire piece is rhythmic, and the largest shell differs only in that it sets a different tempo. This is an excellent example of *variety in unity*.

Wood, reeds, woolen yarn, horsehair, and eucalyptus seeds were combined by Jeannie Freeland to make an extraordinar-

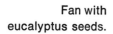

Fan with eucalyptus seeds.

ily beautiful fan. Let's study it to see how the wood and seeds are related to the fiber. The carved wood handle, which has a natural finish, is similar in the dark portion to the color value of the horsehair in the body of the fan. The tone of the lighter sapwood on the left is repeated in the lighter yarns. Notice how beautifully proportioned the area of dark wood is to the lesser area of light.

In color tone the seeds are between the light and dark values in the fan. Their shape repeats the curve of the fan itself. The center of each seed repeats the circle motif of the whole. Their repetition at regular intervals is rhythmic.

The eucalyptus seeds edging the fan.

We can look at the fan and enjoy its beauty without analyzing why it is so pleasing. But when we do think about the way this was achieved, we can use these devices in our own work and we have grown in doing it.

In the swing made by Rosa Kitchen, the wishbone shape of the madrone wood provided the idea for the swing. The

Our rabbit enjoys
Rosa Kitchen's
swing.

forked branches curve to fit a child's body and provide arm-rests. Mrs. Kitchen says that the purpose of the swing is "Magic to keep a very active two-year-old grandson happy and busy in my studio while I'm weaving." The colors are oranges, reds, and yellows, finger-woven and card-woven in strips.

A length of grapevine was used as the actual "loom" on which Dorothy Anne Webber strung some of her warps. Additional warps were added within the body of the weaving. The fact that some of the warps wrap the vine all the way around the form helps in integrating natural object and weaving.

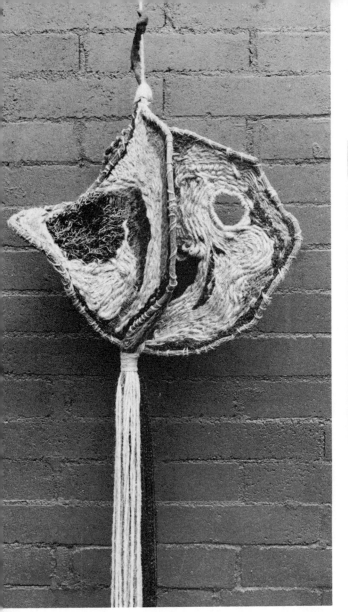

Three-dimensional weaving
by Dorothy Anne Webber.

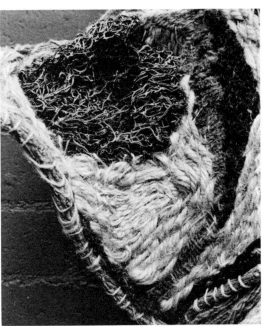

A close-up view of the weaving shows
how some of the warps wrap around
the vine. The rough texture of the
vine keeps them from slipping.

This is usually more successful than simply hanging a weaving from a stick. The curvilineal form of the vine is repeated in the inside circle to which the warps are interiorly secured.

The vine which Mrs. Webber used is called California Wild Grape (*Vitis californica*). It climbs by tendrils to as much as fifty feet into the oaks and cottonwoods of the northern California foothills. In other parts of the country there are other vines which could be used in a similar way. Limber shoots of willow bend nicely. Honeysuckle vines run on for many feet and can be formed as one wishes. Trumpet vines take on unusual curves and they wind around any nearby support and the curves can be utilized in a design.

The grayed blue of the mussel shells in this weaving is repeated in the color of the yarn at the edges. The curved domes of the shells reflect iridescent light in a quiet way. On either side of the grouping coarser yarn is used, emphasizing the shell lines and partly enclosing the cluster. Bringing some of the coarse fiber into the shell area further unifies the weaving.

Mussel shells are used with varied
thicknesses and tones of yarn in Nan Hackett's weaving.

A beautiful beach in Oregon provides Lois Rahkonen with the kelp she incorporates into her weavings. She slices it very thin and allows it to sun until it is thoroughly dry. As she weaves, she nestles the dry slices into areas of similar color value. The off-round shapes which the sliced pieces assume in drying repeat with variation the curve of the circular hoop which frames the weaving. The stem pieces also curve as they dry and are used that way. The colors in this weaving are the blue of the sea and the gold of the sun.

Weaving in a hoop with sliced kelp. (Photo by Alex Murphy)

Eucalyptus bark was the inspiration for Madge Copeland's hanging of irregular shape. The shape which repeats the shape of dappled patches on the tree bark was cut from thin plywood. Pieces of bark, leather, and fur were applied to the

Wall hanging
inspired by
eucalyptus bark.

plywood as well as needleweaving. The needleweaving was
done on a piece of irregularly shaped cardboard. When the
weaving was finished, it was removed from the cardboard and
attached to the wood through holes. The colors are browns
and rusts and grays, all earth tones. From the standpoint of
composition it is interesting to see how the eyes follow through
the central section on the lighter tones in the weaving.

Detail of the hanging showing part of the woven section.

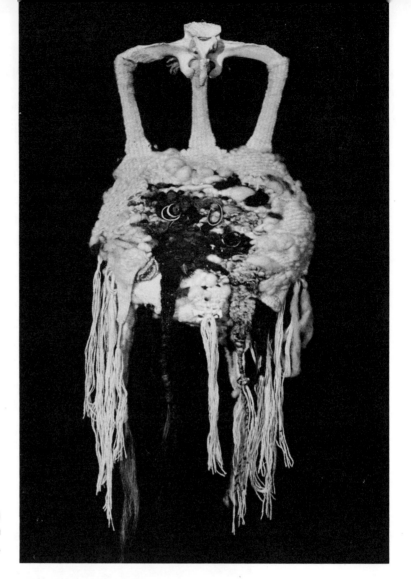

Bones and weaving
combine in
this small hanging.

Bones of all kinds are a special interest of Pat Walls. She
has studied and experimented for a long time with ways of
making them an integral part of her art statements, as she has
done in a hanging. The bone at the top of the hanging merges
so gracefully into the curve of the weaving that the weaving
seems an extension of the bone.

Often natural materials can be most successfully incor-
porated into a work if the natural object is the starting point
and one thinks about how to do something which will be a

setting for the object. A slice of shell was handled this way by
Madge Paro. The interior of the shell is a muted, almost
brownish rose. A piece of suede which is rosy brown was selected as a sort of mounting for the shell. Each color enhances

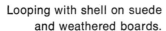

Looping with shell on suede
and weathered boards.

and intensifies the other. Dull-brown weathered boards make the background.

Using Plants as Fibers   Every part of the world has plants which can be used as fiber. Our American Indians were exceptionally clever at discovering ways to do this. The Nez Percé Indians made cornhusk bags which are museum pieces. To soften the husks, legend has it that women chewed them. We have found it works just as well to soak them overnight in glycerin water, a cup of glycerin to a quart of warm water. Cornhusks make a good core over which to coil baskets. Slit them into strips and use these strips in groups to keep an even diameter to the work.

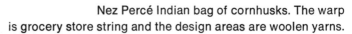

Nez Percé Indian bag of cornhusks. The warp is grocery store string and the design areas are woolen yarns.

Uganda tray made
with banana fiber.

We could conserve paper and cut costs if we carried our own containers to market. In France all the women seem to be carrying little string bags which collapse when they are empty and are no trouble at all to take along when shopping for food. The waste of paper in America is appalling and immoral. We not only save a natural resource when we use reusable containers, we also have the pleasure of handling something made of a natural material. There are few household objects as satisfying as a beautiful wicker basket.

Everywhere there are local plants which can be used as fiber. The people of Appalachia make charming cornhusk dolls, sturdy honeysuckle and willow baskets, woven chair seats of split hickory, and use the juices of plants for natural dyes. It is exciting research to try the things that grow in one's environment. And it is a happy way to make one's own personal revolt against the unfortunate obsolescence that has been built into our economy.

The Africans have been as resourceful as our American Indians in using growing plants for their needs. In Uganda, banana fibers are moistened and wrapped around circles made of coiled grass to form beautiful trays.

New Zealand
flax plant.

Palm leaves are split and spun by rolling them against
the thigh from hip to knee. Splicing is done by overlapping
the ends and spinning them together, making a continuous
filament. Indeed, it would require an entire book just to tell
all of the ways Africans use natural growth for fiber.

In California, a wealth of potential plant fibers grow as
ornamental shrubs. New Zealand flax thrives and can be used
by simply splitting the long, narrow leaves with a pin and

threading them through a needle with a large eye. The basket with lid which we show was coiled by B. J. Koch with strips of flax coiled over thick jute.

The lidded basket of coiled flax over jute.